100

DEAR ANN LANDERS:

"Is there a 100% foolproof way to avoid pregnancy?"

"He loves me and I love him. Why should we deny each other the joy of physical pleasure? We didn't invent these feelings. They are as old as man. Isn't it hypocritical to withhold yourself just because of a lot of old-fashioned taboos?"

"I am 14 years old but my voice hasn't changed yet and I have nothing to shave. Am I a homosexual?"

"Do I have to be a make-out to be popular?"

"I gave him what he wanted and now he won't speak to me. Why?"

These are typical questions from teen-agers who write to Ann Landers!

A kooky generation? No. "A troubled generation," says Ann Landers. "What teens need are straight answers. I believe in our teen-agers and I know that most of them would fly right—if they all knew the score."

> "Ann Landers' wholesome, realistic approach to sex should be as refreshing to the parents reading her book as to their teen-age offspring."
>
> —DETROIT FREE PRESS

Ann Landers Talks to Teen-Agers about Sex

by Ann Landers

FAWCETT 🌺 JUNIPER
NEW YORK

For my granddaughter, Abra Coleman,
who will be a teen-ager in about twelve and a half years

A Fawcett Juniper Book
Published by Ballantine Books
Copyright © 1963 by Prentice-Hall, Inc.

ISBN 0-449-70210-3

This edition published by arrangement with
Prentice-Hall, Inc.

Printed in Canada

First Fawcett Juniper Edition: February 1965
First Ballantine Books Edition: May 1983
Third Printing: April 1986

Acknowledgments

Perhaps I should be ashamed of myself for not cultivating new friends on whom to impose when I undertook to write this book. But who needs new friends when old ones are so durable?

One thing is certain: No writer, living or dead, ever made more unreasonable demands on busy friends and colleagues—and made them twice.

The loyal little band who gave so generously in behalf of my first book *Since You Ask Me* came through again. My warm thanks to the best newspaper publisher a girl ever had—Marshall Field, Jr., for providing me daily with an ideal showcase, *The Chicago Sun-Times*. This remarkable newspaper has given me incomparable exposure plus tender, loving care for eight incredible years.

I can't begin to express adequately my gratitude to Larry Fanning, Executive Editor of *The Chicago Daily News*, who until the fall of 1962 was Executive Editor of my parent paper, the *Sun-Times*. Larry found time not only to produce a newspaper worthy of a Pulitzer Prize but he also continues to edit every word published by Ann Landers. Anyone who benefits from this book is indebted to Larry both for what is *in* it and what is *not* in it.

This gifted Irishman, with his solid judgment

his unerring instinct for the right word, bevels and polishes until what is left is the best of both of us.

Will Munnecke, Vice-President and General Manager of *The Chicago Sun-Times* and *The Chicago Daily News* read the manuscript and jotted down cogent suggestions in illegible handwriting. The Old Grey Fox, with his keen perception, wisdom and uncommon common sense, makes a vital contribution to everything he touches, including this book.

I am deeply obligated to Dick Trezevant, Managing Editor of *The Chicago Sun-Times* for his cool (and sometimes cold) judgments and his forthright criticism. A keen sense of editorial balance makes him an A-1 sounding board.

To Dr. Robert Stolar, Clinical Associate Professor of Medicine, Georgetown University, Washington, D. C., a million long-distance thanks. That's precisely how he listened to this book—one chapter at a time. I am forever indebted to Dr. Stolar for his insistence that I tackle *all* the problems which disturb teenagers. This eminent dermatologist has assured me that what appears between these covers is medically correct.

My affectionate thanks to my nine terrific assistants who kept the ship on an even keel while the book was being written. A 21-gun salute to my principal assistant, Lilyan Simmons for her quiet competence and her staunch Scottish loyalty.

To Jules, my ever-lovin' husband, a pat on his kind, bright head for his saintly patience. After 24 years with this lovely man I am still awed by his beautiful disposition and his mysterious good humor.

A low bow to our daughter Margo Coleman, now a wife and mother, for her assurance that in this book I am not talking down to, or up to, but rather *with* American teen-agers.

Three minutes of silence while I face Pleasantville, New York, and pay homage to Hobart Lewis, Executive Editor and Vice-President of *Reader's Digest*. Hobe responded heroically to my cry for help—and gave a title to this book on the telephone, in 30 seconds flat.

And finally, a word of appreciation to Publishers Newspaper Syndicate and its able president, Harold Anderson, for magnificent efforts in behalf of my daily column. Harold and his colleagues have provided me with a unique opportunity to help millions of people all over the world and I shall be ever grateful for their support.

Contents

Since You Ask Me Again

Dear Ann:

You flatter me by your request for a Preface to *Teen-Agers and Sex,* your second book. No one ever asked me to write two prefaces in a row, but then again no one ever asked me to write one preface either, and anyway, this is the first time you have written two books.

A Preface should explain the purpose, method, or importance of a book, but I have no intention of even attempting to explain the purpose, method, or importance of either teen-agers or sex. You undertake those explanations in your book with greater skill, interest, and authority than I could bring to bear on either subject.

I am, however, a leading authority on the purpose, method, and importance of Ann Landers and address myself to that subject with delight.

Who's Who describes you accurately, though unimaginatively, as:

Landers, Ann (Mrs. Jules Lederer), Columnist; **b.** Sioux City, Ia., July 4, 1918; **d.** Abraham B. and Rebecca (Rushall) Friedman; student Morningside Coll., 1936-39; **m.** Jules W. Lederer, July 2, 1939; 1 dau., Margo. Syndicated columnist Sun-Times Syndicate-Field Enterprises, Chgo., 1955-. Chmn. Eau Claire (Wis.) Gray-Lady Corps. A. R. C., 1947-53; chmn. Minn.-Wis. council Anti-Defamation League, 1945-49; asst.

Wis. chmn. Nat. Found. Infantile Paralysis, 1951-53.
County chmn. Democratic Party of Eau Claire. Mem.
League Women Voters, Brandeis U. Women. Office:
Chicago Sun-Times, Chgo. 6.

While the above is incontestably correct, your
readers should know that Jules is, if possible, an
even more successful businessman than two years
ago when your first book, *Since You Ask Me*, was
published. Your daughter Margo is now the wife
of John Coleman, who is emulating his father-in-
law in the matter of success. And Margo and John
have a daughter, Abra, who will succeed Margo
as Ann Landers after Margo has succeeded her
mother in that role. After all, every dynasty must
have a beginning.

As to your purpose, it is direct and clear—to help
any person make the most of himself in every way
and at all times.

As to your method, it is very simple, yet extremely difficult. You work harder and longer than
any one I know, and harder and longer than you
ever ask of others. You demand the best advice
from experts in every field. You translate the advice of those experts, after seasoning it liberally
with your own knowledge and common sense, into
direct, moving, persuading sentences and para-
graphs.

In brief, you communicate with your readers
with an effectiveness few match and none exceed.

But purpose and method are relatively easy to
describe. The question and the description of your
importance, however, almost call for a "Dear Ann"
letter imploring counsel—almost, but not quite.

For as to your importance, it can be summarized
in one word—*hope*.

You hold hope high before the young and the

old, the strong and the weak, the troubled and the serene. Your readers know you are old enough to understand and to merit the respect of parents, yet young enough to understand and to merit the respect of teen-agers.

Hope is "a person that expectation centers in." You are that person of hope to many. Hope is "trust or reliance" and you are a person of trust and reliance to all.

It is so much easier to begin a Preface than it is to end one. Perhaps the best way to end is to stop—but not until after one more word:

Devotedly,

Wilbur C. Munnecke
Vice President and General Manager
Chicago Sun-Times
Chicago Daily News

one

On Cloud 9
or Behind the 8-Ball

I am the shoulder to cry on. I sit in the watch-bird seat, and it's not difficult to understand why. It's easier to level when you don't have to look a person in the eye and recite the agonizing details of an episode you're ashamed of—particularly if that episode involves a triumph of human chemistry over sound judgment.

For this reason I've been cut in on what goes on behind closed doors and drawn drapes, in the back seats of family cars, on sandy beaches, in wooded lanes—wherever boy meets girl.

Glorious teen-age years! Laughter, fun, popularity, dancing barefoot at proms, exchanging I. D. bracelets, rings, look-alike sweaters, hours of love talk on the telephone, romance under the stars. Pure bliss.

Who says so? Pre-teens, post-teens (with faulty memories), everyone—everyone except the teens themselves. They know better. And I know better, too.

Mountains of mail from the most reliable source of all—teen-agers themselves—tell a different story. A staggering number of teens who appear to be cool, calm and confident, in simple truth, are anxious, frightened and guilt-ridden. They are

15

pulled and hauled by biological urges on the one
hand and fear of the consequences on the other.

First, let's define our terms. Who is a teen-ager?
You may as well ask "Who is man?" or "What
is life?" *Webster's Third New International Dic-
tionary,* which bulks 2,270 pages and cost $3½
million to produce, offers this definition: "Teen-
ager: a person between 13 and 19 years of age, in-
clusive." Big deal!

If Webster's can't come up with a better definition, then what I've long suspected must be true.
There is no such animal as a typical teen-ager. He
can't be defined because he doesn't exist. Yet we
can scarcely pick up a magazine or a newspaper
which doesn't have an article on "What Teen-
agers Want" or "What Teen-agers Need" or—
worst of all—"The Moral Decay of the Youth of
America."

Adults who talk about teen-agers in unhar-
nessed generalities do all our kids an injustice.
Teen-agers are not lima beans. They are human
beings who come in assorted sizes, shapes and
colors. Each has his own personality, his own sense
of personal worth and his own moral and ethical
value system.

The difference between age 13 and age 19 can
be 100. I've received letters from 15-year old girls
who have had so many sexual experiences they
can't recall the names of all their partners. In the
same batch of mail I might receive half a dozen
letters from 16- and 17-year-olds who want to
know if it's possible to get pregnant through clothing.

Although there is no typical teen, my mail tells
me an astonishing number of high school kids
share common problems. They are either on Cloud

9 or behind the 8-Ball about eleven times a week. They alternately love and hate their parents. They want more freedom on the one hand, yet on the other they desperately hope Mom and Dad won't let them do every fool thing they beg to do. They struggle with acne, overweight and underweight, and the sweet and frightening mysteries of awakening biological drives. They're bedeviled by pesky brothers and sisters, wail over impossible math courses, and hunger to be popular.

They die when they are left out. They want to be exactly like everybody else—right down to the skinny pants, the beat-up sneakers, the bulky sweaters or whatever happens to be "in" at the moment.

Alexander Graham Bell is their patron saint. To the teen-ager the telephone is vastly more than an instrument of communication. It is an emotional outlet. The tinkle of this magical gadget can send a 15-year-old into ecstasy. A silent phone can plunge a teen-ager into the cellars of despair.

One thing is certain. After 12 and up to 20, life is not easy.

A KOOKY GENERATION?

Are teen-agers today wilder than their parents were at a comparable age—or are they just getting more public attention? I am asked this question frequently, particularly by parents. They usually put it this way: "Are our children worse than we were when we were their age?"

I don't like the word "worse." The teen-agers of today are *different* from teen-agers of thirty years ago. My answer is not based on memory. It is based on statistics. Anyone who has been working with young people since World War II will tell you that more teen-agers are in trouble today —more serious trouble, and at an earlier age— than ever before. And it isn't just that there are *more* teen-agers.

The percentage of adolescents in trouble is up. What are the reasons? Have today's teen-agers invented a new kind of mischief? No, they have not. They are doing, essentially, the same things their parents did—but they are doing them sooner. And this is where the trouble comes in. *Since World War II, the timetable of sex activity among teen-agers has been set ahead by approximately three years.*

When I was a teen-ager (back in the Stone Age, of course) 13-year-old girls didn't wear nail polish, nylons, strapless evening gowns and lipstick. A 14-year-old boy who smoked usually did it behind the barn. There wasn't the social pressure to "grow up." Our mothers didn't worry so much about whether or not we were popular. Back in the 1930's, mothers were worrying about other things —like how to feed their families.

Of course we were interested in sex. (It's obvious that the interest in sex has been fairly high for some thousands of years.) But my generation was more self-conscious about it. In our day, 16-year-olds hugged and kissed and called it necking. Today most 16-year-olds go beyond hugging and kissing, and they call it "making out."

It is substantially more difficult to be a wholesome teen-ager today, and, to some extent, the reasons are economic. The "under 20" group spends nine and a half million dollars a year without adult supervision. Teens are stimulated by advertisers to buy more—and to want more. Advertising suggests that the way to be popular is to rev up the sex appeal. Sex screams from the billboards. Cigarette ads show kids lolling in the grass. The hi-fi and stereo ads show kids on the floor. The sun lotion ads show kids on the sand. Everybody is lying down with someone.

Most of our newspapers and magazines glamorize the escapades of movie stars, particularly people's husbands or wives. Some metropolitan newspapers printed a full page of pictures of half-nude (and well-known) lovers locked in an embrace on the deck of a yacht. The heroine of this real-life drama is married—but not to him, and she is the mother of three young children.

Small wonder our teen-agers get a cockeyed view of morality when such garbage can find a ready market in some of America's "best" newspapers. These are the gods and goddesses their elders have given them to worship.

More than any single factor in the past thirty years, the automobile has exerted the strongest influence on teen-age behavior. Millions of teen-agers own cars—and those who don't own a car can often get four wheels on half an hour's notice.

A car today is more than transportation. It is a status symbol and a passport to freedom. Six gallons of gas can propel a couple of teen-agers into another world. A car can be a portable bedroom —"even with those crummy bucket seats," as one teen wrote.

Today's automobile has all the comforts of home, plus privacy. The radio provides mood music. The glove compartment can accommodate a few cans of beer or a bottle of booze. If it's cold outside, you can turn on the heater. If it's hot outside, you can turn on the air-conditioner.

Nature's wonders can be glorious and stimulating. Safe in a car you can watch the stars twinkle in the heavens, listen to the howling wind or the gentle patter of the rain. With a set-up like this, it's not surprising that half the kids who write and say they are in serious trouble admit it happened in a car.

Am I suggesting teen-agers should not be allowed to have cars? I am not. That would be absurd. Cars are built into twentieth-century life. We can't turn back the clock or the calendar, nor should we wish to.

I *am* strongly suggesting, however, that teen-agers should recognize that a car presents multiple temptations which can add up to deep trouble. Even the most disciplined boy or girl is battling against brutal odds when he parks in the moonlight—"just to talk."

A kooky generation? No. A troubled generation, struggling not only with the problems of growing up but with the added pressures of the space age—a generation forced to live in a world it never made. But what new generation ever made the world it came into?

two

What about
Going Steady?

For several years I've had a running debate with my teen-age readers about going steady. I am against it, and I continue to be against it, although I've been told repeatedly that I'm out of my mind.

The high school polls—and I've seen dozens, from Fairbanks, Alaska, to Harlingen, Texas, from Augusta, Maine, to Eureka, California—prove that you teen-agers have already decided the double-harness arrangement isn't the living end.

There are some temporary social benefits to be gotten out of going steady, but in my book the disadvantages clearly outweigh the advantages.

I asked a number of Chicago high school boys who are going steady why they prefer the steady arrangement to free-lance dating. Their answers demonstrated that going steady meant something quite different to each of them. Here are some of the reasons the boys gave for dating one girl exclusively:

J.R.: "It's cheaper. When you take out a different girl every weekend, you have to spend money to impress her. With a steady you can sit at her house a lot and it doesn't cost anything."

B.P.: "I'm sort of bashful around girls. It took me six dates to get up enough nerve to hold this

one girl's hand. It took nine dates to kiss her. Now
we are making out pretty good. I'd hate to have
to start all over again with somebody else."

S.D.: "I guess you might call it love. I think
about Debbie an awful lot. When I am with her, I
feel great. She's the only girl I have ever felt this
way about."

C.E.: "My folks say it isn't decent to take out a
different girl every weekend. They won't let me
have the car or spending money unless I stick to
one."

B.D.: "Let's face it. A guy has to have a sex
life. If a guy goes steady with a girl, it's a lot easier
because then everything is settled. You aren't
arguing about it."

Going steady means something quite different to
this boy from Canton, Ohio:

"Dear Ann Landers:

"I am 17, a senior in high school. I was
never very good in athletics, and I always
hit the books pretty hard. My grades are
good and I play the cello in the school or-
chestra.

"I've always been shy around girls so when
Vera invited me to a turn-about dance (that's
when the girls ask the fellows) I was pleased.
Vera is a nice girl but a little on the heavy
side. I've got a lot of pimples on my face so
I figure that makes us even.

"Three weeks after the turn-about dance
I invited Vera to the Junior-Senior Pow-
Wow. We had a great time. The next day
at school Vera suggested that we go steady.
All this means is that we are both sure of a

date when something important comes up at school.

"We are not in love—in fact, I have never even kissed her. Our steady deal is good for me because it means I won't have to break the ice with some girl every time I want a date.

"Yesterday our principal made a long-winded speech against going steady. Most of the stuff he talked about didn't apply to Vera and me at all. We are going steady technically maybe, but not like most of the kids in school.

"I am writing this letter just to explain a point of view that some people don't seem to understand. Best wishes.

Shy Guy"

And now that we've heard from the boys, let's examine the female point of view. Girl's go steady for a variety of reasons also, but usually it's because:

(1) They are in love with Mr. Wonderful and don't want to go with anyone else.

(2) They lack confidence and are afraid to compete for dates in the open market. Going steady, they claim, insures social security. It is the not-so-popular girl's vaccination against "stay-at-home-itis."

Another female type (and one of the worst) is the ego-feeding head hunter.

The head hunter must continually prove to herself, and to the world, that she is a *femme fatale.* She collects boys like some girls collect autographs. She announces with considerable fanfare that she and Rickey are going steady. Two weeks later she has ground Ricky into mincemeat, and she is going steady with Wilbur. Poor Wilbur lasts 10 days and is then sentenced to the slaughterhouse with Rickey. Don is her next victim—I mean steady— and then comes Bob. Jack is next—and so on.

Her bedroom is a veritable museum of love relics—stuffed bears, stuffed pandas, stuffed kangaroos—all testimony to her claim that she is indeed a killer. She will tell you unashamedly that she went steady with seventeen fellows from April through June.

An unusual version of going steady is described in a letter from Davenport, Iowa:

The mother of a 10-year-old girl wrote to ask what to do about her daughter, Dora, who seemed prematurely preoccupied with the opposite sex. One day Dora came home and announced at the dinner table that she and Freddie were "going steady." Freddie is the freckled-faced kid, age 10, who lives next door. The stunned mother asked Dora,

"What do you mean by 'going steady'? Where do you *go?*"

Dora replied, "Oh, we don't really go anywhere, Mother. He just hits me during recess."

Another mother writing on the same subject:

"Dear Ann Landers:

"I am a mother who does not agree with your position on going steady. My daughter is 13 years old and in the seventh grade. She is going steady with a very nice boy of 14 and I am delighted. Last year when she didn't have a steady boy friend she was a terribly unhappy girl. She was always worried to death she wouldn't be invited to this party or to that ball game. It was a sad sight to see this child teary-eyed and fretting, waiting for the phone to ring. Going steady means nothing more to a seventh grader than having somebody to count on. Please don't be so hard on these 13-year-olds, Ann. Things are different than when you and I were teen-agers. Today it's a serious thing for a girl to be dateless.

R. D."

I replied:

"Dear R. D.:

"And who made it a 'serious thing' for a 13-year-old to be dateless? Mothers like you. The divorce rate is going through the roof—largely because of half-baked, premature marriages. When mothers prime their 12-year-old daughters to be man-traps, the kids become so jaded and bored at 17 there is nothing left to do but get married. At 19 there's no place to go but to the divorce court. Please keep my address handy, Mother. I have a sneaking suspicion you'll be writing again.

Ann Landers"

When R. D.'s letter and my reply appeared in print I received a reply from Donald Pownell, executive director of Fairhaven, a home for unwed mothers in Sacramento, California:

"Dear Ann Landers:

"*R. D.* was wrong in her first sentence. She wrote, 'I am a mother.' She is a female baby-sitter, and a poor one. A mother should have some maturity. When talking of her 13-year-old daughter, she said, 'It's a sad sight to see this child, teary-eyed and fretting, waiting for the telephone to ring.' Ask her, Ann, if she thinks it is pleasant to see 12- and 13-year-olds sitting teary-eyed and fretting—pregnant in a maternity home. They tell us that going steady was the cause. We get some girls who are 11 years of age. I have seen them and I know what I am talking about.

"*R. D.* says things are different than when she was a girl. There she is right, Ann. Things are different. The unwed pregnancy rate is more than 300 percent higher. Five years ago we had empty beds. We added a unit recently, and still we have room for only one out of four applicants. Many of the girls who come to us tell us Ann Landers sent them. Please keep hammering away in your column about the dangers of going steady. From where I sit things don't look good."

A going steady variation to which I am strongly opposed is the "You belong to me and I belong to you" type. These couples see each other at school every hour of every day. They walk to and from classes together. They have lunch together. They have a standing date for every weekend, which means Friday and Saturday nights and Sunday. Distance and parents permitting, they sometimes see each other during the week.

A strict hands-off policy is observed by other fellows and girls. It is clearly understood that steadies go to all school functions together. It's total togetherness. They are as close as pages in a book and this closeness is advertised to all the world.

Why am I opposed to it when it all sounds so positively dreamy? For two reasons:

First, going steady cheats you of the opportunity to learn about *all* kinds of people. It is an insulated sort of existence which can plant you in a rut—and the only difference between a rut and a grave is in the dimensions.

Dating years are precious. They are years during which you develop patterns and techniques for dealing with people. A free-wheeling dating arrangement will give you confidence and teach you social skills. The challenge of adjusting to new situations will keep you alert. The ability to get along with all types of personalities—even the wacky ones—will be a valuable asset throughout your life.

The person who wisely avoids the paralysis of going steady has an opportunity to hone his wits against the sharper wits he encounters. He learns to be patient with the crashing bores. He gains insight into the behavior of others. And he discovers from experience (sometimes painful) that there are degrees of integrity, loyalty and dependability. Only by dating a variety of people is it possible to make meaningful comparisons.

The mature, well-rounded adult is the sum and substance of everything he has ever read, every project in which he has participated and every individual whose life has touched his.

It is inevitable that you will become involved

with the activities of the person you are dating. Going steady with a boy who is an expert at skeet shooting is dandy—you may become a crack shot yourself. But if you had gone with ten other fellows as well, you might have gained some understanding of ham radios, photography, football, politics, jazz, Bach, woodcarving, folk singing, comparative religions and psychoanalysis.

Going steady is like settling for one outfit when you could have twenty. It is like listening to the same record endlessly when you could be listening to fifty. It cheats you of limitless experiences and adventures. This is a big price to pay for what many teen-agers call "Social Security."

Even the brother-sister, no-pulse type of going steady, as described by Shy Guy, is a second-rate idea. Shy Guy professed no emotional attachment to his steady girl. He described their relationship as a convenience rather than a romance. Although this type of going steady sounds perfectly harmless, it is undesirable because it is self-defeating.

Shyness with girls reflects a fear of competition and a feeling of inadequacy. The bashful boy *needs* the experience of dating several girls. Only then will he acquire confidence.

The following excerpts from teen-agers' letters express eloquently the value of free-lance dating.

From Houston:

> "I went steady with Bill all through my freshman year. He was a sweet guy but not very interesting. For three months I wanted to break up with him but I was afraid to. No other fellows showed any interest in me and I was scared I'd be sitting home alone.

When I finally got up the courage to make the break, I realized what I had been missing.

"All sorts of fascinating guys turned up out of nowhere. I was like a girl who had very bad eyesight and didn't know it. When she finally got a pair of glasses, she became aware of things that had been around her all the time, only she couldn't see them."

Hartford, Connecticut:

"I went steady with Martha for two years. She was sort of like my mother—bossy and like that. Martha was always telling me what to do. Finally I got fed up on her bossiness and I let her know it. It wasn't until I began to date other girls that I learned all women weren't that way."

San Bernardino, California:

"I went steady for eight months and decided I'd had enough. My first two months of freedom were like a nightmare. I hit an unbelievable run of jerks. But I learned something—even from them. I learned that it takes a lot of self-discipline to be gracious and pleasant when you're trapped with a loser. If I marry a fellow who has a boring boss, I will know how to cope with the situation."

Phoenix, Arizona:

"I am going steady with Ron but to be honest about it, I would like to break up with him. He wants to be with me every minute. I feel like I'm in jail. I'm losing all my girl friends because of him. He gets sullen and pouts when I tell him I want to be with Louise or Sue on a Saturday afternoon. He is even jealous of my cousin Ted. He resents it when I have to go somewhere with my folks."

Winnetka, Illinois:

"I went steady for over a year with a kid who used to impress people by breaking $10 bills to buy cokes. I didn't realize it when I was going with him but this was smart-aleck stuff. When we broke up I began to date a few fellows who had to carry their lunches and who work on Saturdays. I learned there is more to life than riding around in a convertible and sitting in reserved seats for a Bears game."

Grosse Point, Michigan:

"There are five girls in our crowd who are real close. We tell each other everything. Three of these girls are going steady.

"Each of these three girls, within this past year, was worried to death she might be pregnant. And yet they don't see anything wrong in what they are doing. They all say they plan to marry their steadies eventually so that makes it all right."

And this brings us to the most dangerous by-product of going steady.

It is unrealistic to assume that healthy, red-blooded high school kids can be together, day in and day out, month after month—sometimes year after year—and keep their physical urges under perfect control. I am not saying it is impossible, but I *am* saying it is unlikely. Some teens write to say they put up a hectic battle, but time and chemistry proved to be too formidable a combination. There is no denying that when the irresistible force meets the immovable object, something has got to give—and usually it's the "immovable" object.

three

How to
Break Up with a Steady

My mail tells me that at least 25 percent of the kids who are going steady would like to break up, but they don't know how to go about it. I've learned the following lines by heart:

From Longview, Washington:

"I liked Kathy a lot at first and felt lucky when she agreed to go steady with me. I'm ashamed to admit I talked her into doing things she didn't think were right. Now I feel like a dirty skunk because I've lost interest in her. A new doll has moved here from Seattle and I'm dying to take her out. How can I ditch Kathy without hurting her feelings?"

From Eau Claire, Wisconsin:

"Sid and I used to have a ball together, but he's no fun anymore. You'd think we had been married 25 years. He never dresses up for me like he used to and he doesn't even notice when I have a new hairdo or a new dress. All he wants to do is sit around my house or park at Half Moon Lake. When we first started to go steady, he said he loved me and I said I loved him. At the time I really meant it. Now that my feelings have changed I feel like a hypocrite. I can't find the words to tell him."

From Honolulu:

"Mike and I have been going steady for three months. We haven't gone the limit yet, but I don't see how I can hold out much longer. Every time we park I promise myself I'm going to make him behave, but when he kisses me I get weak all over and my good intentions fly out the window.

"I've got to break up with him because frankly he's not the kind of guy I want to marry. He hates school and has no ambition. I'm sure he'll never amount to anything. Please don't think I'm terrible, Ann, but I'm drawn to Mike for purely physical reasons. I know it's wrong and dangerous. I know what I should do but I need someone like you to tell me I *must* do it. Please help me."

There are as many reasons for wanting to break up with a steady as there are reasons for wanting to go together. Whatever *your* reasons for wanting to break up (the most common one is "I just got tired of him—or her"), I urge you to do it promptly. The longer you postpone a dread task, the more dreadful it becomes. So once you've decided to chop it, get going.

Please don't attempt to do it by letter or telephone. This is the coward's way out. Tell him to his face, And tell him *first*. Nothing is so devastating or hurtful as hearing via the grapevine that your steady is about to dump you.

Pick an appropriate time and place. Timing and surroundings are important. Don't tell him on the eve of a big exam or on the way to the Senior Prom, or during lunch hour when others may be milling about and the bell may ring at any moment. And above all—be kind. Remember that words are weapons. Choose them wisely. There are dozens of ways of saying the same thing. Spare him.

Breaking up a close relationship is bound to be awkward at best and agony at worst. If two people have meant a great deal to each other, the farewell can be loaded with emotional fireworks. Often there are feelings of guilt, anxiety, shock and even betrayal.

Often steadies who continue to go together past the time when they should have called it quits get on each other's nerves. They're either at each other's throats or they quietly bore one another to death. Neither knows for sure what happened to the Great Love Affair of the Ages. Perhaps it died of natural causes. Instead of facing this simple fact and giving the romance a decent burial, the couple keeps going together only because it's easier than facing the ordeal of splitting up. These couples are not sweethearts. They are more like a pair of matched mules.

The most explosive bust-ups are between couples who have had a 200-watt romance and then, somehow, a third party got into the act. This brand of "unfaithfulness" is against the code, of course, because "we were almost as good as married and how could he do this to me?" The final battle is usually rough, and both combatants wind up deeply wounded. Every shred of affection is destroyed, and the two people who once meant a great deal to each other wind up hating each other.

When the break-up is one-sided, as it often is, somebody feels discarded. The individual who is performing the social surgery should, in the name of mercy, use an anesthetic when he severs the ties. The "Flake off, Buddy Boy, you bore me" farewell is unforgivable. The girl who can't resist turning the handle after she has plunged the knife between his shoulder blades often pays a dear price for her moment of "satisfaction."

Maturity and *consideration* are two big and important words. When breaking up with a steady, then, may I suggest that you review the positive aspects of your friendship—the good times you have had together—and spell out your appreciation of his or her fine qualities. Make the point that you are depending too much on one another and that such dependency is unhealthy for you both. Explain that you feel it would be better if you dated others. You might mention the possibility of picking up the threads later, after each of you has had a chance to play the field and make comparisons.

A first-rate guy who wants to break up with his steady allows her to save face. It is humiliating for a female to get the ax publicly, so a gallant fellow spares the girl embarrassment by making it appear as if the break-up was *her* idea. The boy who does it this way loses nothing, and he gains the undying gratitude of the discarded sweetheart.

Terminating a close relationship in a civilized manner is a measure of maturity. Consideration for others (in addition to being a virtue in itself) is a prudent investment for your future peace of mind. We all know people whose lives are hopelessly cluttered with corpses of dead romances. They are haunted by bitter memories of love affairs with nightmare endings. The girl who is unable to enter a room without encountering half a dozen former heartthrobs to whom she is no longer speaking cannot help but regret her brashness. The boy whose farewells have been shoddy and cavalier earns for himself the reputation of a heel.

When the romance is over, both parties are honor-bound to keep quiet about whatever went on between them. Nothing is so despicable as the blabbermouth who spreads the word that his ex-girl friend was a "push-over" or a "hot number."

The girl who circulates damaging reports about her former boy friend does a serious disservice to herself. If he was such a jerk why did she go with him? She advertises her own poor judgment.

When the break-up comes, don't allow your temper or your hurt feelings to turn you into a hand-painted polecat. The highest tribute is to have it said of you—"We used to go together and I've never known a finer person. We always will be good friends."

four

Why Not Go all the Way?

Oliver Wendell Holmes said, "No generalization is worth a damn—including this one." So let's avoid generalities and get to specifics. It isn't enough anymore for a mother to tell her 16-year-old daughter, "Nice girls don't do that." Her daughter may just happen to know some nice (but stupid) girls who do.

What am I saying? That a girl can be nice even though she goes all the way? Yes. The girl can be nice—but the girl is not very bright. I may be criticized by religious leaders for taking this position, but those who hope to frighten teenagers in line with hell-fire speeches had better wake up and smell the coffee—because the kids aren't buying.

Religious training and strict adherence to moral codes may keep *some* teen-agers from going across the line, but too many teen-agers want other reasons. The lofty concept that virtue is its own reward "makes a nice embroidered sampler—to be framed and hung in grandmother's kitchen" wrote one teen-ager. Even the lovely word "chastity" has an old-fashioned ring to it—like "chaperone" or "Minuet in G."

Only a fool would tell a teen-ager to stop thinking about sex. You may as well tell the sun to stop shining. Teen-agers *are* thinking about sex, and they will continue to think about it. What they need is sound information so they will know *how* to think about it.

For too many years the subject of sex among teen-agers was soft-pedaled. There was a widely held theory that frank discussion might excite undue curiosity. "Don't give the kids ideas" is the way it was put. Well, the kids already *have* ideas, and many of them have put the ideas into practice. Adult silence serves only to widen the gap between two generations which are already too far apart. I am a strong advocate of open discussion—and the more open the better.

The cold, blunt facts are these: I know from the hundreds of letters I get each week from young people that a shockingly high percentage of high school students, by the time they reach their junior year, have had some experience with the opposite sex. By "experience" I mean more than necking and petting. I mean sexual relations.

Most boys view sex differently than girls. The boy in his teens rarely sees any connection between sex and love. He often has no emotional investment in the girl. He is merely responding to his biological urge. His attitude is: "Why not? A normal guy has to."

It is not uncommon for a teen-age boy to use sex as a "proving ground" or a prop for his ego. He may try out a girl just to see if he can make the grade because he has heard other boys have.

Sex is frequently used not only by teen-agers but by adults as an escape from a world which they find difficult and demanding. Sex provides them with momentary excitement, a feeling of importance and even power. It diverts the mind from the central problem—a nagging feeling of inferiority—real or imagined. In other words, some people use sex as others use alcohol or narcotics.

Teen-age girls who indulge promiscuously in sexual relations do so for a number of reasons. Some girls foolishly believe it is the key to popularity. They fear if they refuse to give the boys what they ask for, the boys will not invite them out again and will turn to someone who is more accommodating.

And then, of course, there is the pitiful little mouse who has no confidence in her ability to hold a boy's interest. She believes the only way she can show a fellow a good time is to allow him to take liberties with her body.

The girl who goes steady is frequently pressured into sexual experimentation by her boy friend, who persuades her it's the way to "prove your love." Girls who write to me with this problem get my stock answer:

> "Tell him no dice. Ask him to prove *his* love by exercising some manly self-control. A boy who makes such demands on a girl is not interested in *her*. He is interested primarily in satisfying his own selfish desires. Sex relations outside of marriage prove nothing—except that the people involved had neither the self-discipline nor the good sense to wait."

Another ever-present hazard of sexual relations is venereal disease. I have devoted a later chapter to this problem because it is a serious one among teen-agers—and one which, unfortunately, is too rarely discussed because of a naïve conviction that "nice" people don't get VD. (See chapter seven.)

The young girl who has a long list of sex partners is emotionally disturbed and needs professional help. Such girls often come from homes where the father is absent because of death or divorce (or he may as well be absent because of his coldness and indifference). The girl who is starved for male affection yearns to feel a man's arms around her—any man's arms. So she becomes an easy target for any fellow who happens along. Sometimes these girls don't even wait to be asked. They aggressively seek sex partners.

Another reason for promiscuity among young girls is rebellion against excessively strict upbringing. The 16-year-old girl who is not permitted to date or receive telephone calls from boys and is warned steadily about the evils of sex, may sell her family the idea that she is "Little Goody Two Shoes." But when she escapes from home for a few hours, she is determined to do all the things her parents have ordered her not to do. Her bizarre behavior is her protest against what she feels is cruel and unjust treatment.

The heartbroken parents of these girls write very sad letters indeed. These lines from a Toronto mother are typical:

"We can't understand what happened to Betsy. She is 17 and has never been allowed to go with a boy. We watched her very closely and knew where she was every minute. She told us last night that she is in a family way and doesn't even know the boy's last name.

My husband and I are sick at heart. Where did we fail?"

Most teen-age girls who have sex relations before marriage are filled with romantic fantasies of one sort or another. They identify themselves with heroines in love novels or with movie actresses or with adults they believe are leading exciting lives. Usually the girl persuades herself that the boy cares a great deal for her, so what she is doing really isn't wrong after all. If they're going steady, she tells herself, "I'm crazy about him and we plan to get married eventually so it's perfectly all right."

These girls don't escape the guilt, even though they attempt to justify their out-of-bounds behavior to themselves and sometimes to others. They verbalize the notion "It's perfectly all right," but the carefree façade is only a pose. These girls know (and suffer from the knowledge) that society does not approve of their behavior and that they are living outside the bounds of convention.

Call it "narrow-minded," "mid-Victorian," "puritanical" or whatever may come to mind, but sex outside of marriage is unacceptable in our society. This conflict can play havoc with the nervous system—and often does.

Some young girls who write me declare that chastity not only is out of style but unrealistic. They attempt to relieve themselves of personal guilt by pointing a finger at society and declaring, "*I* am right. *You* are all wrong." They insist that the moral codes are antiquated and that society is deaf, dumb and blind because it does not accept what is "perfectly natural."

Such reasoning is, of course, filled with fish

hooks and booby traps. But it's the best they can do, and they play it to a fare-thee-well. The following letter expresses this point of view:

"Dear Ann Landers:

"I am a high school senior who will be 18 in four months. I read your column every day and I think you dig teen-agers. This is why I am writing to you.

"Can you tell me why it is wrong for two young people who are in love and who someday plan to marry to have premarital relations?

"My boy friend and I have been going steady for 16 months. We are faithful to each other. He loves me and I love him. Why should we deny each other the joy of sexual pleasure? What do we gain? We didn't invent these feelings. They are as old as man. Isn't it hypocritical to be in love and withhold yourself just because of a lot of old-fashioned taboos?

"At first I fought against it and finally I couldn't see any reason to keep fighting so I gave in. I'm glad I did because now I feel like I really belong to him. Please tell me, Ann, why does society say this is wrong?

Debbie"

Debbie got her answer in the mail. And if you don't know what the answer is, you'll find it in this chapter.

A great many young girls have sexual relations with their steady boy friends, believing that they will be married one day and, therefore, nothing is sacrificed.

These same girls often write to me later with this question:

> "Can a fellow tell if a girl is a virgin? I gave myself to a boy I went steady with because I was sure he would be my one and only. Now we have broken up and I am worried sick that the man I marry will know I didn't save myself for him."

I tell these girls that sometimes a man can tell and sometimes he can't, but the less said about the past the better. When a girl marries, she has a right to expect her husband to judge her on the basis of her behavior with him. No man should insist on a white-flower girl unless he is able to bring to the marriage the same credentials of purity.

Now let's get down to cases. What *is* wrong with going all the way? Aside from the moral issues (which too many teen-agers have long since discarded as being out-of-date), the best reason is this: *It isn't worth the risks.* Sex outside of marriage is a bad bargain when you measure what you stand to gain against what you stand to lose.

What are the gains? Popularity? Nonsense. The pushovers may get a flurry of attention, but it doesn't last long. The word gets around, and soon the free and easy "make-out" has a rotten reputation. The boys may phone her when they are in the mood for fun and frolic, but this is a far cry from popularity. Better call it availability.

What is left then? The pleasure of the act itself? Exactly how much pleasure is there for illicit beginners? *Do* teen-agers find sex as heavenly and as exciting as they thought it would be? The answer is NO. It's likely to be a disappointment.

A clinic which serves unwed mothers in a large Eastern city made an interesting study of premarital sexual relations. This question was asked of the unwed mothers: "Did you find the sex experience pleasurable, disappointing, or unpleasant?" Only 20 percent described their sex experience as pleasurable. The other 30 percent described it as unpleasant or revolting.

Most teen-age boys, because they think of the sex act as something "to do and get over with," are not satisfactory love partners. They are undisciplined and awkward. They lack patience and understanding. Sex on the sly can turn one of life's most rewarding experiences into a hideous nightmare.

Lovemaking, when it must be conducted on the Q.T., is generally uncomfortable and hurried. When two people sneak around fearful of interruption or of being caught, the sex act is rarely satisfactory, much less beautiful.

Often girls write to tell me of their deep disappointment. They thought it was going to be the most glorious thing that ever happened, but instead it made them feel cheap, dirty and disgusted with the boy as well as with themselves.

Now, what can happen to teen-agers who become involved sexually? Many things. And they don't always happen to *other* people. Sometimes they happen to you.

Speaking specifically: Girls get pregnant. And in the last 20 years the percentage of unwed mothers has tripled. I don't mean *number*—I mean *percentage*. And this includes only the unwed mothers in registered homes. The unmarried girls who have abortions or can afford to "go visit relatives in another state" will never be known.

In 1961 one out of every eight girls who married was 17 years of age or younger. An educated guess indicates that approximately 40 percent of these girls were pregnant when they married. The divorce rate for brides under 20 is three times the average for all age groups.

And it is a matter of record that the so-called "adult" marriages aren't doing so well. According to the statisticians, one out of every three couples who marry today will be looking for a divorce lawyer within five years.

Teen-agers who sample the physical pleasures of marriage would do well to consider *all* the possibilities. The kids who figure "if something happens we can always get married" had better understand what this means. Too often it can mean broken-hearted parents, a sudden end to education, and being saddled with responsibilities of manhood and womanhood at a time when you should be enjoying teen-age fun. And you can wind up hating your wife or husband.

Here is a letter which describes the situation:

"Dear Ann Landers:

"I am 17 and already my life is messed up. Ted and I went steady for six months and we began to do things we had no right to do. I became pregnant.

"We both quit school and got married right away. My folks thought it would be best if we moved out of town, so we did. I hate my life and what I have done to Ted. The baby

cries all the time and gets on Ted's nerves.
He drinks too much and I can't blame him. We
live in a dump and there is no money for
sitters or movies or decent clothes. Ted never
says anything but I know he must hate me
because I got him into this. I'm afraid he
hates the baby, too. He never holds her or
pays attention to her.

"There are times when I think this is all a
bad dream and I'll wake up at home in my
own bed, and get dressed and go to school
with the kids I liked so much. But I know too
well that those days are over for me and I am
stuck.

"I'm not writing for advice. It's too late
for that. I'm just writing in the hope you will
print this letter for the benefit of other teen-
agers who think they know it all—like I did.

Wrecked at 17."

What can I say to this young girl? Can I tell her
she was a fool—that she made some bad decisions?
She knows all that. What a terrible price she is
paying for her mistakes! Yet this girl didn't do
anything that many teen-agers have not already
done. But they have been more fortunate—so far.

Some girls find false security in this line: "If
something happens to you, honey, we'll get married right away." The following is from a 16-year-
old girl who learned too late that this phrase can
be part of the Big Sell and that the boy has no intention of making good his promise:

"I let him have his way because I was in
love with him and didn't want to lose him.

When I told him I thought I was in trouble, he said, 'Gee, that's tough. My dad would kill me if he knew I was mixed up in something like this. You're on your own, kid. I hope you get along O.K.'"

Every now and then I get a letter from some knuckle-head who tells me if I really want to befriend teen-agers, I should give them some helpful hints on how to avoid pregnancy instead of being so doggone puritanical and unrealistic.

To you teen-agers who think you can "get away with it" if you are careful, I would like to say this:

There is no 100 percent foolproof, sure-fire way to avoid pregnancy. Anyone who thinks so is sadly mistaken. Every procedure designed to prevent conception has some flaw. Some techniques are less risky than others, but none can be depended upon to be 100 percent secure. Teen-agers should be fully aware that every time they indulge in sexual relations they take a chance on bringing another human being into the world.

Even married couples who have everything going for them, including competent medical advice, have "accidents." Young, inexperienced kids who must sneak and hurry to indulge in forbidden activity under undesirable conditions take far greater chances.

Teen-agers who are having sexual relations should ask themselves one question: "What will we do if the act should result in pregnancy?"

I am well aware that some teen-agers are not in trouble at this moment—and they will never be in trouble. They are the level-headed and clear-eyed ones who have grown up with the knowledge that the human body has dignity and that the pleasures of the body have a higher purpose. Such teen-agers are not in danger of fouling themselves up.

No one can go along on dates with you and see that you stay in line. The best policeman of all is your own set of standards. The most dependable of all compasses are still common sense and good judgment. We must make our own decisions—and our own choices.

five

How to Help Yourself
Stay Out of Trouble

The word "teen" comes from the Old English word "teona" which means grief, misery and pain. This bit of background may be comforting. It should help to know that teen-age years have always been rough.

I was under the impression that life for teenagers was a breeze—until the time had come for *me* to be a teen-ager. Then the sky fell in. The year was 1931. The country was paralyzed by a devastating depression. I had persuaded myself that my teen-age difficulties were in some way linked with the financial condition of the country. It wasn't until later that I learned prosperity didn't make teen-age life any happier.

The process of growing up is painful because growing means changing, and changing means pain. It helps if we can place the blame for our failures and inadequacies on something or someone outside ourselves. I had the depression to blame. Fifteen years later teen-agers had World War II. Today, it's the H-bomb.

Some troubles are beyond man's ability to control. Among the most obvious are birth deformities, serious illness, the loss of loved ones, flood, fire and just being hit by a falling brick. Call it

49

tough luck if you wish (heaven knows some of us have more tough luck than others) but *all* of us, if we hang around this planet long enough, are destined to get some cuts and bruises.

If we are honest we will admit that we bring certain agonies right down on our foolish heads. The secrets of contentment include the capacity to accept with grace the bumps we cannot duck and to avoid the bumps which are avoidable, and the wisdom to distinguish between the two.

Man was not meant to be a sitting duck, vulnerable to any and every kind of misfortune. God gave man the gift of will and the power of reason and the mental equipment with which to make choices.

But no matter how efficient the mental machinery may be, no one makes precisely the right decision every time. Even the smartest ones goof. Most teen-age-type troubles don't "just happen." We ask for them. The following letters from my reader mail illustrate the point:

Kenosha:

"I never should have had all those drinks. If I hadn't been crocked I wouldn't be in this mess. I'm so ashamed I can't look my mother in the eye. But I'll have to tell her—and soon. Please send me the name of a home I can go to, a place not too far from Kenosha. I'd rather not be right in town."

Los Angeles:

"It was a warm night. Somebody suggested going down to the beach for a swim. It seemed like a great idea. Nobody had a swim suit, naturally, so the fellows went in wearing their shorts and we girls wore our bras and panties. After all, as the boys pointed out, bikinis are being worn almost everywhere and they are skimpier than bras and panties. That swimming party went on until after 2 A.M. Then the couples began to wander all over the beach, in different directions. I guess it must have been because we didn't have much clothing on, but my boy friend and I lost control of our emotions and you can guess the rest. I don't know yet if I am pregnant, but if I am my father will kick me out of the house."

I think you get the idea. If you want it in a neat little package, here it is: Don't overmatch yourself. When you plop yourself right square in the middle of a tempting situation, you are begging for trouble. Unchaperoned, moonlight beach parties, for example, are loaded with dynamite. So are unchaperoned picnics, ski parties, hunting and fishing excursions—anything that brings two people close to nature and takes them a million miles from the eyes of civilization and stills the voice of reason.

No self-respecting (or smart) girl accepts an invitation to her boy friend's house when she knows his parents are out of town. Nor does she invite him to *her* home under similar circumstances.

And if your parents have not set a curfew for you, then set one for yourself. The girl who can stay out as late as she pleases invariably stays out too late. Fellows sometimes gripe about "strict" rules and regulations, but in truth, a first-rate boy has little respect for a date who can be picked up at the corner drug store and dropped off at a girl friend's home at any old hour. A girl puts a cheap price tag on her company if she is available for as long as the boy wants to keep her out.

As for unchaperoned parties, I am against them. A couple of adults, or at least one parent, should be somewhere under the roof when a teen-age party is in session. I don't mean Mom and Dad should park themselves in the center of the activities and police the action, but at least one adult should be on the premises, and the kids should know it.

This in no way spoils the fun. It does provide a safety-valve which can be a godsend when a couple of dozen high-spirited kids get together. The parents of the teen-ager who is giving the party owe simple prudence to the parents of the kids being entertained. An invitation to a teen-ager's home should carry with it the assurance that it will be a safe and wholesome evening. Parents who permit their teen-agers to have the gang over and then go off and leave the kids to do as they please are not being fair to other parents.

I often hear from young mothers who engage sitters. They ask if it's advisable to permit a sitter to entertain her boy friend while she is on the job. The answer is a firm NO. The sitter is being paid to take charge of the house and children in the absence of the parent. The girl who is employed in an office or in a shop would not presume to ask for the privilege of entertaining a guest. The sitter has a responsibility to her employer to devote her undivided time and attention to the task for which she was hired.

Some sitters refuse to sit unless they are permitted to entertain on the job. The girl who insists on such fringe benefits is probably using her job as an excuse to do things she can't do in her own home—and I recommend hiring another sitter. Here's an illustration:

A Connecticut mother had engaged a sitter from 7:30 P.M. until midnight. When she and her husband returned home about 11:30 P.M., the sitter and her boy friend were in the den. The hi-fi was going full blast, and they were dancing.

The three-year-old boy had gotten out of bed, climbed on a chair in the bathroom and removed several bottles of pills from the medicine cabinet. The parents were unable to determine whether he had swallowed any pills so they rushed the child to the hospital and had his stomach pumped out.

Had the sitter not been entertaining her boy friend, she might have heard the child moving about upstairs or checked him periodically to make sure he was in bed where he belonged.

Teen-agers who have no specific plans and cruise around aimlessly often wind up parking beside the road "to talk." And parking can lead to serious trouble.

Remember—double-dating statistically reduces the chances of becoming intimate. That couple in the front seat or back seat can be darned good insurance against going too far. Some high schools have a rule which prohibits freshmen and sophomores from single dating. Exactly how such a rule can be enforced I cannot say, but it's a sound idea and I heartily endorse it.

Up to now we have discussed staying out of trouble from the negative point of view. We have emphasized what *not* to do. Now let's see what positive steps can be taken.

First, accept your sexuality. Don't try to deny

it, and don't be ashamed of it. It's good. At the same time you must understand that sexual drives create physical tensions. These tensions build up and become more insistent in their demands for expression. Damming up tension produces anxiety, frustration and even physical discomfort. If you direct this energy into wholesome, constructive channels, you will burn it up instead of letting it burn *you* up. Athletics is one of the healthiest and most satisfying outlets. The teenage boy who has had two and a half hours of basketball or football practice or a couple of hours on the tennis court is less likely to be riding around in the evening looking for girls.

Any physical exertion is useful, but equally useful is a fascinating hobby, something that requires concentration and will keep you busy.

A recent study included this question, which was addressed to teen-agers (ages 13-18): "What do you do with your spare time?" Almost 88 percent of the teen-agers who had been in trouble with the law answered "Nothing."

Housework, particularly floor-scrubbing, is not only great for the female figure, but it's good for the soul. And it will help take the edge off your sex appetite. Cooking, baking and sewing will prepare you for homemaking. Energy siphoned off into these constructive channels will leave less energy for preoccupation with erotic fantasies. (They called it being boy-crazy when I was a teenager.)

Of course you would not be normal if you were able to keep your mind off the boys, completely. And no normal boy is able to keep his mind off girls *completely* either. The old-fashioned idea that boys and girls who were kept busy would forget all about each other is a lot of eye-wash.

Sex education has not advanced generally in the last 25 years. But progress has been made in the honest discussion of masturbation. I can document it in my reader mail. I receive surprisingly few letters from teen-agers who are worried about masturbation. The letters expressing deep concern come from ignorant parents. Sample:

"I am afraid our 16-year-old son is practicing self-abuse and I'm worried sick that it will make him feeble-minded."

Medical authorities tell us that masturbation is a normal part of growing up. Almost all boys and at least 75 percent of the girls practice self-manipulation at some time or another during adolescence.

Masturbation is more common and more frequent among boys than girls because boys are more readily excited by visual images. A boy can become aroused by looking at a picture of a half-clad girl or by seeing a girl in a tight sweater. He can become excited by touching her bare leg or her bare back. A boy's desires may be triggered by a sexy story or by just daydreaming about a girl and imagining what it might be like to make love to her.

Females are not so affected by such stimuli nor are their sex fantasies so vivid. Girls are inclined to be more romantic than physical—they relate sex to romance and love rather than to biological urges. Obviously there are exceptions among both boys and girls. General condition of physical health, the rate of metabolism and the way the glands function play a vital part in regulating sex appetite.

Masturbation does *not* cause pimples, acne, a sallow complexion or dark circles under the eyes. Masturbation will *not* stunt the growth, cause sterility or insanity. People who are mentally ill sometimes practice masturbation, but this is not what brought on the illness. It is *not* true that young people who masturbate do not later have satisfying sex relations in marriage.

I have received letters from adults who tell me they masturbated during adolescence and have continued the practice after marriage. This does not mean masturbation during adolescence destroyed the individual's capacity to enjoy a normal sex relationship. It does indicate, however, that something is drastically wrong with the couple's sex relationship. No mature person would prefer self-gratification to intercourse.

All the authorities I have consulted tell me the only serious damage which results from masturbation is the shame and guilt which young people feel in connection with the practice. There are known cases of teen-agers who committed suicide because they were unable to stop the practice and they decided they were too evil and too weak to go on living.

It is well to remember that even though self-manipulation will not cause you to lose your mind as our grandparents thought, it is a negative and childish habit. The teen-agers who feel they are sinning against God when they indulge themselves (some religions consider masturbation sinful) express in their letters a pathetic sense of worthlessness. I make an attempt to urge those individuals to live up to their religious teachings. If their religion can provide them with the strength to abstain I applaud both the kids *and* the religion.

As we grow into manhood and womanhood and as our concepts of love become more meaningful, we should understand that for genuine sexual satisfaction, we must feel a deeper need to give than to receive. Real fulfillment is found only in a love relationship which involves another person. It cannot be found in solitary physical pleasure. This is why God made man *and* woman.

six

Booze and You

This chapter is not going to be a sermon on the horrors of alcohol. Each of us knows dozens of respectable people who drink and enjoy it. Liquor has never been a problem to those people, and it never will be. They have never lost a day's work because of drinking—although an occasional hangover may have made them wish they had put the cork back in the bottle a few drinks earlier.

These respectable social drinkers live useful and productive lives. And they will probably die of natural causes without having seen even one pink elephant.

From the beginning of recorded history man has used alcohol. Using certain roots and herbs, or berries and fruit, he found that through fermentation he could produce a liquid which made him "feel pretty good." This elixir was believed to possess magical powers because those who drank it behaved as if they were under a spell. It was used primarily in religious ceremonies to drive out evil spirits.

After a while people began to work up their own little mixtures for personal use. Obviously, the idea caught on, because in 1962 (in the United

States alone) more than five billion dollars was spent on hard liquor.

Let's face it. Liquor is here to stay. For those who hoped otherwise, the signal rang out loud and clear when the Prohibition Act of 1920 laid one of the biggest social eggs in history.

The Eighteenth Amendment, forbidding the manufacture and sale of intoxicating beverages (except for medicinal and sacramental purposes), did not change people's drinking habits. It drove people underground. They couldn't drink legally, so they drank illegally. "Moonshine" by the barrel was manufactured in backyard stills. Bathtub gin was downright fashionable. Thousands of people went blind from wood alcohol.

The Prohibition Act fathered a billion-dollar business, bootlegging. Rival gangs pumped each other full of lead, and many a rum-runner wound up at the bottom of a river—wearing a cement kimono.

The sale of liquor was clearly against the law, but everybody knew where to get a bottle, or a couple of jiggers of Scotch served in a coffee cup. Finally, our legislative leaders were forced to concede that Prohibition was a national joke. Not only did Prohibition fail to reduce drinking, but probably it had increased it. A new attraction had been introduced—glamour. Americans who otherwise would not have dreamed of getting drunk were lured into speakeasies "just for the heck of it—it might be exciting."

In 1933, to the surprise of few Americans, Prohibition was repealed. The electorate decided that in a free country people have the right to get slopped to the eyeballs if they want to—that it is both undemocratic and impossible to dictate to adults what they may or may not drink. The Eighteenth Amendment was repealed, and the bootleggers had to go back to legitimate work.

Although the sale of liquor to minors is still illegal, every high school kid knows how and where to get it. So, like every other question that involves human behavior, to drink or not to drink must be resolved at the personal level. Each of us must decide for himself what to do about it. People who lead well-ordered and productive lives think ahead. They anticipate situations and problems, and they decide in advance how these situations and problems will be met. If you have some vague, half-baked notions about whether to drink or not to drink, it is likely that you will fall victim to your own indecisiveness.

It would be unrealistic to write a book on teenagers and sex and ignore drinking, when thousands of teen-agers have told me that liquor was one of the major causes of their sexual involvements.

Before we explore the effects of alcohol on the personality let's examine some of the evidence that tells us what alcohol does to the body. Moderate drinking (and by moderate I mean two or three drinks on a Saturday night) will have no permanent, damaging effect on a normal, healthy person. Two drinks may interfere with vision and coordination just enough to cause a serious auto accident, but this is a different matter.

Moderate drinking will not rot the liver, the stomach or the kidneys, nor will it lead to deterioration of the brain. Remember I am using the word *moderate,* and I refer to normal, healthy people. This does not include those who are allergic to alcohol. Some people should have *no* liquor. They are alcoholics. For the alcoholic one drink is too many and one hundred is not enough.

The drinker who starts early in life multiplies his chances of becoming a problem drinker. A Yale University study on alcoholism shows that at least two-thirds of the known alcoholics began drinking while in high school, or even sooner.

What then is liquor good for?

A medicine? The folklore that liquor is useful for medicinal purposes is for the most part scientifically incorrect.

More folklore: Liquor can cure a cold. The fact: It usually makes a cold worse.

The old wives' tale that alcohol should be kept on hand in case of a snake bite is malarkey. In this emergency I suggest the liquor be poured on the snake. (Just remember that if you are ever bitten by a snake, don't take a drink, because alcohol will dilate your blood vessels and spread the poison through your system more rapidly!) These facts are *not* folklore:

Alcohol is useful as a sedative. It slows up the body processes, induces drowsiness and sleep.

Alcohol is also useful as a pain-killer. In fact, alcohol and ether are similar in chemical composition. The formula for alcohol is C_2H_5 OH; the formula for ether is C_2H_5 O C_2H_5.

Some physicians recommend a drink before dinner to stimulate appetite. But this would scarcely be of interest to teen-agers, since most teen-agers have appetites which could usefully be curbed, not stimulated.

I have asked hundreds of high school kids why they drink, and these are the most common reasons, among both boys and girls:

"When everybody in the crowd has a drink I

don't want to be different. Some kids call you chicken if you're the only one who won't join in."

"When I take a drink it makes me feel grown-up."

"A drink releases me and makes me more friendly. I guess you might say it loosens me up socially and I'm not so self-conscious."

"When I'm in a blue mood or disgusted about something, a few drinks give me a lift and make me forget."

Let's examine this magic elixir and how it works to produce these feelings. Almost everyone who drinks will swear on a stack of Bibles that liquor stimulates him. Exactly the opposite is true. Liquor unquestionably produces a superficially stimulating effect, but the exhilaration is only temporary. Liquor is a depressant—as any doctor will attest.

Why then, after a few drinks, do people often become friendly, lively and even boisterous? How can a few ounces of liquid produce feelings of exhilaration, superiority, self-confidence, power?

The answer is simple, once you understand the chemical nature of alcohol.

Alcohol goes to work on the area of the brain which controls reason, judgment and our inhibitions. That area of the brain then tends to become less effective than it normally is. It is "frozen." If a dentist has ever given you a shot of novocaine, you are familiar with the feeling of numbness that follows. The dentist can extract a tooth after an injection of novocaine, and you will feel nothing. Alcohol works in much the same way.

The personality changes that occur as a result of excessive drinking mystify and terrify relatives and friends of problem drinkers. They don't know what to make of it or what to do about it:

"Dear Ann Landers:

"Can you tell me how two drinks can turn a lovable, intelligent, well-mannered, considerate young man into a crude, vulgar boor? The person to whom I refer is very dear to me. It breaks my heart to see this frightening change in him. From a gentle soul he is transferred into an incorrigible trouble-maker. Last week he was arrested for disorderly conduct. He started a fight in a public place.

"If he drank a great deal of liquor I could understand it but he goes crazy on two highballs. What can I do to help him? Thank you for any advice you can give me. I am desperate.

Myrtle"

I replied:

"The young man you are writing about is an alcoholic. With these sick individuals the amount of alcohol consumed makes little difference. Some alcoholics go off the beam after one drink. An alcoholic should not have even one drop of liquor. Urge him to get outside help. Alcoholics Anonymous and Portal House are excellent organizations. Look under Alcohol in the telephone book."

Frequently a person who drinks is under the impression that liquor brings out his attractive and admirable qualities, unleashes his flashing wit and transforms him into an interesting conversationalist. Liquor can indeed produce some radical personality changes, but whether these changes are for the better can be decided more accurately by a sober (and objective) observer. Alcohol cannot improve talent nor can it bring out hidden genius. It can only fog the judgment and display a raw, uninhibited personality.

The feeling of being on top of the world is temporary. When the drinker moves past his threshold of tolerance the rosy glow fades and the drinker often becomes depressed, miserable, ill—and sometimes loses consciousness.

The aftereffects of a booze blast can be devastating. Although no one has ever died from a hangover, a great many people have wished they could. The morning-after feelings of nausea, weakness, remorse, and guilt can be overwhelming. Added to the physical misery of a hangover, the anxiety of being unable to remember what was said or done is pure torture. Many worthy people have lost fine jobs and destroyed valuable friendships because of boorish and revolting behavior triggered by too many drinks.

Some unconscionable males who are aware that liquor breaks down resistance will try to get girls to drink so they'll be more amenable to suggestion. Dorothy Parker's couplet is well-known to the wolf pack: "Candy is dandy, but liquor is quicker."

This is how the booze trap operates. The shy girl will take one drink to conquer her self-consciousness. She tells herself, "I need something to relax me. I'm all tied up in knots. One drink will help." And that *one* drink may well jolly her up a bit. She becomes friendly, even affectionate—sails about the room buoyantly, saying delightful things. Through her Scotch-tinted glasses the world looks glorious.

If one drink can produce such lovely feelings, she reasons that two drinks will make her feel even better. So she takes a second drink—and a third. The outcome of the evening is anybody's guess, because after four drinks the poor girl is no longer in control of her senses. This pathetic letter from Oklahoma City describes such a situation:

"Dear Ann Landers:

"I am so sick of myself I could just die. Please tell me if there is any way I can repair the damage I have done.

"Last night one of the greatest guys in school took me to a party. It was my first date with Jim, and I had been hoping for six months that he would ask me out. Jim travels with the best class of kids in school because he is tops in athletics, has a car of his own and is a big wheel. I wanted to make a knockout impression on Jim as well as the other kids who were there.

"I was nervous, naturally, so I thought one drink would loosen me up a little and give me the courage to speak to people. Well, I overdid it. I drank a little of everything—first a couple of martinis, then I switched to Scotch and soda. I don't know how many drinks I had, but pretty soon I began to feel weak and dizzy. I couldn't make it to the bathroom and got sick right in the hall. I heard the hostess say to Jim, 'Don't ever bring that rum-bucket to *my* house again.' He answered, 'No danger. After tonight I wouldn't take the idiot to a dog fight.'

"I don't remember much that happened after that. I recall putting on my coat, and Jim took me home. The next day at school I saw some of the kids who were at the party and they were sort of cool. Jim drove by when I was walking home. I'm sure he saw me but he kept right on going. I'm so ashamed of myself I'd like to fall in a hole and stay there forever. How can a person live down such a terrible mistake? Is there anything I can do to square things with Jim? Please help me.

Louise"

Of course it is impossible to undo what has been done, but no "terrible mistake" is without value if you learn a lesson from it. The tragedy of too many drinkers, however, is that they *don't* learn a lesson. Their compulsion to drink is stronger than their decent intentions. Their insecurities compel them to reach for a crutch. They go right on drinking, telling themselves "I can handle it." And they hate themselves in the morning.

Why are liquor and sex frequent and natural bedfellows? Because liquor has the power to break down the will and paralyze the judgment. Teenagers (and adults) who write me often confess they first became involved in illicit sexual relations while under the influence of alcohol. They say, "If I hadn't gotten tanked up I wouldn't be in this mess. I'm really not that kind of person—and never have been. After a few highballs I lost my head completely."

Let's explore the link between sex and liquor. The sex drive is one of the most powerful and persistent drives known to man. Through the centuries civilized man has learned to control his primitive urges. This is one of the basic differences between human beings and the lower animals. But when liquor gets into the act, the inhibitions melt away and animal instincts take over.

The sex urges are present whether you are married or single, drunk or sober, deeply in love or just cruising around in search of a little excitement for the evening. The biological drive is concerned only with reproduction and is ever alert for the opportunity.

Frequently I receive letters from young girls who think they may be pregnant but are unable to remember if they had sexual relations. This letter from Buffalo is typical:

> "I'm worried to death and I can't talk to anyone else about this problem. I think I am pregnant, but I can't remember if I did anything wrong. I always thought beer was harmless and that a person couldn't get drunk if he stuck to beer. I know I had three cans of beer but after that things got hazy. My boy friend was drinking beer with vodka chasers. I remember arguing with him about the wild way he was driving. The next thing I knew I woke up at home, and I can't recall another thing about that night. I've tried to find out from my boy friend what happened, but he doesn't remember anything either."

How can a teen-ager best handle situations which might result from excessive drinking? This is how I dealt with the problem when I was a teen-ager.

I looked around at the kids in my school who were drinkers. Some of them were fairly well thought of, they came from respectable families and were not what you'd call hoodlums. But they were, for the most part, the hell-raisers, not the leaders or the kids I admired.

Then I observed what went on at parties. I believe this, more than anything, led me to the final decision. The top-notchers, I noticed, were navigating under their own power. They were having every bit as much fun as the kids who were getting stoned, but there was no sweat. They avoided liquor without making a point of it.

I watched the kids who were drinking. Their antics ranged from the amusing to the revolting. As the evening wore on, moods changed. Some of the kids became depressed and sullen. Others became pugnacious. The girls who drank too much were the saddest sights of all. Their hairdos collapsed and makeup which had been painstakingly applied was smeared and running. I often thought if someone would take candid pictures and show them to these girls the following day, it would dry 'em up forever.

An appropriate caption for the panel of photos could be the words of Robert Burns:

> Oh wad some power the giftie gie us
> To see oursels as others see us!
> It wad frae monie a blunder free us,
> An' foolish notion.

The *big* problem in drinking seems to be knowing when to call a halt. I concluded it was a lot easier not to take that first drink than to burden myself with deciding when to quit. So my drink was always ginger ale, or tomato juice or orangeade. And it still is.

Did being an abstainer label me a square? (In those days the term was "wet blanket.") Did it interfere with my popularity? I don't think it did. I always had plenty of boy friends—in fact, I suspect being a nondrinker increased my popularity because I was a "cheap date." The boys didn't have to spend much money on me because my liquid intake for the evening was two ginger ales.

Now and then there was a little needling... somebody would ask if Carry Nation had brought her hatchet. But I never took the digs seriously, and I doubt that anyone else did. I have never felt that being "dry" made me better or worse than anyone else. My decision not to drink was based on reason. I noodled it out, and the choice had nothing to do with religion or moral principles. I believe the decision was a good one and that perhaps it saved me some unhappy moments and even some grief.

The teen-ager who decides not to drink owes neither an explanation nor an apology. He is in effect saying, "This is *my* way of meeting the situation and it's my own business. I like the way I am. I don't need to search for confidence or self-assurance at the bottom of a bottle. I don't need liquid assistance to pep me up, to enhance my personality or to make me one of the crowd."

Some teen-agers—and surprisingly enough, more adults—feel compelled to drop a cherry in their 7-Up so that it will appear to be a Tom

Collins. They feel they must cover up the fact that they are drinking a nonalcoholic beverage. On occasion it has been suggested that I use this decoy so the ginger ale will look like the "real thing." I've been told it will "make others more comfortable."

Nonsense.

I refuse on the grounds that if their drinking doesn't bother me, my *not* drinking shouldn't bother them.

I've given you the facts on drinking, as I see them. It's up to you to decide whether to take the wet road or the dry. To those who choose the dry route, I hold my glass of ginger ale high and offer a toast, "Congratulations, and welcome to the Club."

seven

VD Is Not
an Adult's Disease

This is the chapter I was advised not to write. One well-intentioned friend said, "VD is a medical problem. You are not a physician. Stay away from it." Another friend warned, "The subject is too sordid—not a subject *you* ought to discuss. Parents will read the book and be furious with you. Why borrow trouble?"

When someone cautioned me to "stick to emotional and social problems," I knew that the chapter was going to be written. For what is more social than gonorrhea and syphilis? I know of no better way to be of service than to give correct information on important subjects in language people can understand.

When I told a 20-year-old girl I was preparing a chapter on VD for a book addressed to teen-agers, she replied, "I didn't know teen-agers got VD. I thought it was an adult's disease."

Medical science in recent years has discovered drugs which can eradicate venereal diseases—and quickly. There need not be even one case of VD. But obviously the answer does not lie in medication alone. All of us must be educated to understand the nature of the diseases, how they are contracted, how to recognize the symptoms and what to do when the symptoms are recognized.

Teen-agers have to be told that venereal diseases can be deadly and destructive if untreated. They must be conditioned to speak the words gonorrhea and syphilis as readily as they speak the words tuberculosis and pneumonia. The subject must be taken out of the back alleys and latrines and brought into the living rooms, the lecture halls, and, yes—even into the classrooms.

We have come a long way since Bernarr McFadden was sentenced to two years in prison and fined $2,000 for mailing a magazine containing an article on venereal diseases. In 1909 President William Howard Taft saved McFadden from prison but McFadden had to pay the fine. We have come a long way, indeed, but we have a distance to go.

Now, a word to parents: If you believe VD is not an appropriate subject for teen-agers, have a statistic: *Every study shows that more than 50 percent of male VD patients became infected for the first time between the ages of 15 and 19!*

Dr. Ralph W. Tyler, of the Center for Advanced Study in Behavioral Sciences at Stanford University, told a VD conference in Chicago, "Since 1957, there has been a sharp increase in infectious syphilis in persons under 20 years of age. The increase in one year—1961 over 1960—was 56 percent." Dr. Tyler suggested that at least an additional 25 percent of the cases were not recorded because many private physicians do not report VD. Dr. William J. Brown of the U.S. Public Health Service in Atlanta recommended that VD information should be given in the classroom, no later than the seventh grade.

The rising rate among teen-agers is not confined to American boys and girls. At a meeting of the World Health Organization in Geneva, it was revealed that there has also been a sharp increase in the incidence of venereal disease among teen-agers in Mexico, Denmark, Sweden, France, India and Great Britain. The Soviet Union has an unusually low VD rate. Dr. N. M. Ovchinnikov of Moscow explained the reason: A Soviet citizen who becomes infected and fails to cooperate with public health authorities can draw a prison sentence of up to three years.

Most states require a blood test for all couples who wish to marry. Every day I receive letters from readers who ask for a list of states which do *not* require a blood test. These people harbor the ridiculous idea that the condition of their blood is nobody's business but their own. Or they suspect they have VD and want to keep it a secret.

Such stupidity is criminal. A compulsory blood test may well be a nuisance, and some misguided fools may consider it an invasion of privacy; the state, however, is not remotely interested in our private affairs, but the state *is* properly interested in protecting unborn children.

A syphilitic father cannot pass the disease on to his child, but he can infect his wife and *she* can pass the disease on to her baby. A pregnant woman who has syphilis should be treated. If she does not receive treatment, her baby may be born dead, deformed, deaf, blind or paralyzed. Every pregnant woman should have a blood test immediately upon learning she is pregnant. If she has syphilis and is treated before the fifth month, her chances for giving birth to a normal, healthy baby are excellent.

Why the increase of VD when medical science

has given us the drugs with which to eradicate it? Unfortunately we have become less vigilant in case-finding. Physicians and clinics have eased the drive which was prevalent 15 years ago against VD. The overconfidence produced by the miracle drugs is partly to blame.

In addition to this, sociologists tell us that children grow up faster these days. They date earlier and are tempted on all sides to sample adult pleasures. Teen-agers have cars, money, leisure time and less supervision. Sex is glamorized and teenage drinking is on the increase. Add it all up and you have the formula for Instant Trouble.

In 1943 when Dr. John Mahoney reported the successful use of penicillin in the treatment of syphilis it was hoped that this was "the answer." Within a few years it was apparent that "the answer" had hatched a new set of problems. A great many people reasoned that the miracle drugs reduced VD to an annoyance—no more dangerous than the common cold. A few shots could cure it, so why worry? Public health support was sharply reduced because of the fantastic number of cures in the rapid-treatment centers.

VD—who are the candidates? I have received hundreds of letters from teen-agers and adults who describe VD symptoms but insist they couldn't possibly have contracted one of the diseases because their friends are so "nice."

Let's get one thing straight: *Germs know no class lines and plenty of "nice" people do get VD —and they pass it on to other "nice" people.*

A 15-year-old girl who lives in Harrisburg, Pennsylvania, wrote that she had little sores on the intimate parts of her body. She said the itching "drove her crazy. But," she added, "I just couldn't have a venereal disease because I've gone all the way with only one boy and he is my steady. He's a very refined young man and comes from a well-to-do and prominent family. He couldn't have given me anything like *that*."

A 17-year-old boy from Memphis wrote:

"I am writing to you because I can't talk to my folks about this problem. I've heard the guys in the locker room laugh about gonorrhea. They always make a big joke of it. I'm afraid I may have it but I can't figure out how it happened. I've had quite a lot of pain. At first I thought I strained myself playing football, but other things have happened which makes me sure it must be something else. I only go out with girls from good families. I have never been with a prostitute or a tramp. The four girls I have had relations with all go to my church and are very high-class."

Every day my mail brings me dozens of similar letters from teen-agers who "think they may have something" and beg me to tell them what to do. Invariably they add, "I can't tell my folks. They would die of the shock."

Here are some facts every teen-ager should know about VD:

(1) Gonorrhea and syphilis are the most common venereal diseases, but there are three other types which usually remain local and do not spread through the body as do gonorrhea and syphilis. These three local types of VD are called chancroid, lymphogranu-

loma venereum and granuloma inguinale.
They produce sores in the region of the sex
organs, and there is often severe swelling
of the groin. Chancroid may be painful, the
other two are not. These three more obscure
venereal diseases must be treated medically,
just as gonorrhea and syphilis are treated.
They do not disappear or "wear themselves
out—like a common cold."

(2)   Gonorrhea and syphilis can be crippling and
even fatal if not treated.

(3)   The VD rate is always higher in the lower
socio-economic groups. There is a clear cor-
relation between VD and people who do not
have equal opportunity for education, employment and social justice. But there are
no racial characteristics which make one
group of people more susceptible to VD than
another.

(4)   VD *can* be cured. The earlier the treatment
is begun the better the chances for a complete cure.

(5)   It is possible to have both gonorrhea and
syphilis at the same time. Having one does
not immunize against the other.

(6)   Once cured, a patient can contract the disease again if he is exposed to someone who
has it. The records show that 80 percent of
those who are infected will become re-
infected in the future—probably one-fourth
of these people within six months.

(7)   It is *not* true that VD is passed on only one
way—through sexual relations. The overwhelming majority of VD cases *do* result
from sexual relations with an infected per-

son, but medical journals have recorded many exceptions.

It is extremely unlikely that VD will be caught from towels, toilet seats, contaminated drinking glasses, silverware, and so forth. But no one can say for sure that it is impossible. There are recorded cases of virgins who have contracted syphilis and gonorrhea.

Dr. Robert Stolar, a dermatologist and syphilologist of Washington, D.C., reported the case of a fellow physician who contracted syphilis while performing an autopsy on the corpse of a syphilitic. The doctor accidentally tore a small hole in his rubber glove during the examination. There was an open cut on his finger. The infection entered the bloodstream through the hole in his glove. The doctor didn't realize he had been infected until several weeks later when a sore appeared on his finger. He became suspicious when the sore did not heal after a few days. A blood test (which is called a Wasserman reaction, named after the doctor who developed the test) proved to be positive, indicating syphilis. The doctor was stunned. It required hours of searching his memory before he was able to piece together the details—the autopsy on the syphilitic, the hole in the rubber glove and the open cut on his finger.

SYPHILIS—HOW CAN YOU TELL?

The first sign of syphilis is a sore which usually appears where the germ entered the body. It can appear on any part of the body, but often it is around the sex organs or the mouth. This sore is called a chancre; it is pronounced "shanker." A chancre resembles a rather angry pimple, or a cold sore. The chancre usually appears from 10 days to three months after the individual has been exposed to the disease.

In some cases no chancre appears—or it looks so innocent it is ignored. Chancres are not painful but sometimes they produce itching. When the chancre is deep inside the female sex organs it cannot be seen or felt.

These are the first symptoms. *They will disappear without treatment. This* is why syphilis is a vicious and dangerous disease. The infected person who does not recognize the first symptoms is unaware that the infection is at work in his body. Even though the sores disappear, the germs multiply in his system and travel through the bloodstream, performing their deadly, destructive work.

About three to eight weeks later, the secondary symptoms appear. Often what is mistaken for hives or a heat rash shows upon the skin. Sores frequently appear in the mouth or on the palms of the hands and soles of the feet. The palm and sole sores are frequently mistaken for callouses. Headaches may occur. Sometimes the hair becomes thin and lifeless, or it may fall out in patches. Kissing during this stage can infect another person.

These secondary symptoms will also disappear without treatment. If the disease is not recognized and treated at this stage, however, the infection becomes well entrenched and begins to do permanent damage to the heart, the blood vessels, the brain and the nervous system—as well as to other vital organs.

During this time the victim may feel perfectly well and function normally—not missing work, school, church or social functions—until the heart or the nervous system becomes seriously damaged. And some may become blind, hopelessly crippled, or insane.

Today the treatment for syphilis is a series of injections of penicillin or other antibiotics. These shots are painless. It is not unusual for a patient to have a negative blood test after one or two shots. This does not mean he is cured and can discontinue treatment. It does mean, however, that he cannot pass the disease on to someone else. The full treatment for syphilis is a minimum of ten shots; these shots may be given within a period of ten days or spaced three or four days apart.

After the treatments have been concluded most doctors insist on a blood test every three or four months for two or three years. This is to insure no recurrence of the infection. Sometimes the disease will be arrested and not show up in a blood test for several weeks, then suddenly it may become active again.

CAN IT BE GONORRHEA?

Gonorrhea is almost always contracted through sexual relations, but physicians have reported exceptions. There have been recorded cases of virgins who have been blinded by gonorrhea. The eyes are especially susceptible to this infectious germ.

Gonorrhea in the female is difficult to diagnose early because there is no pain or discomfort. The infected female does not feel ill. The only symptom is a discharge from the sex organs. Pain occurs only after the disease has become fairly well ad-

vanced. When it invades the female tubes, gonorrhea can cause sterility. It can also cause heart
trouble, crippling arthritis, blindness and sometimes death.

In the male, gonorrhea is easier to diagnose because the symptoms are more dramatic. Anywhere
from three to ten days after the male has become
infected he may notice a discharge from the sex
organs and a burning sensation during urination.
The discharge becomes heavier as the disease pro-
gresses. The pain begins soon after, in the area of
the groin. Pain sometimes becomes so severe that
that patient is incapacitated. If gonorrhea is untreated in a male, the spermatic tubes are affected
and he may become sterile. He may also develop
heart trouble, crippling arthritis and blindness.

Gonorrhea is treated by injections of penicillin
or other antibiotics. Two or three shots can cure
an active case. For chronic gonorrhea the treatment is more intense.

How To Protect Yourself Against VD

Since the overwhelming majority of VD cases
are contracted through intercourse, the surest
way to protect yourself against VD is to avoid
heavy necking, which so often leads to sexual relations.

As I pointed out earlier, there is a chance VD
can be picked up by kissing an infected person,
so I urge you to be alert. If your steady or your
date has what appears to be a cold sore, don't kiss
him. If the sore persists for several days, urge the
individual to see a doctor, and tell him why. If he
refuses, then you ought to stop seeing him. If you

have sores in your mouth, do not kiss anyone—
relative, friend or sweetheart. If the sores do not
disappear within four or five days, see a doctor.

People who read about symptoms often imagine
they have the disease, be it polio, TB or VD. But
if you have never had sexual relations, the chances
are about 1,000 to 1 that the cold sore on your
lip is only a cold sore and nothing more. If, however, you have had sexual relations and you recognize a combination of the symptoms described in
this chapter (and that cold sore seems stubborn
about healing), don't be a fool and let fear keep
you from seeking medical help.

I suggest three courses of action, depending on
your home situation and your relationship with
your parents.

(1) If it is possible to discuss problems of an intimate nature with your mother or your
father, by all means tell them that you want
to see your family doctor immediately—and
why. It may be plenty tough to face your
parents with this blockbuster but please
look at it this way—if you have VD you will
not be cured without treatment. Delaying
treatment will give the infection an opportunity to become more firmly entrenched.
And you have a moral responsibility to
others. An infected person who is not treated
may infect members of his family or his
friends.

(2) If you feel you cannot discuss the problem
with your mother or father, please go to
your family physician. Some states require
physicians to notify parents of all medical
procedures performed on minors. Other
states do not. When teen-age readers tell me

they are unable to talk to their parents I
suggest that they go to see the family doctor.
Many teen-agers have written to thank me
for the suggestion and usually they've reported that the doctor agreed to respect
their confidences. These teen-agers paid for
the treatment themselves, out of their al-
lowances, baby-sitting money, and so forth.

(3)   If you cannot face your parents with the
problem and are not on friendly terms with
your family doctor, go to the city or county
health department. (Refer to the phone
book.) Ask to see a doctor. Tell the doctor
you think you have VD. If you are under
16, they may contact your parents. If you
are 16 or over and you ask them *not* to contact your parents, they may respect your
wishes. I cannot guarantee this, but in many
cities teen-agers are treated for VD and
their parents are not notified. Most city and
county public health clinics will treat VD
patients without a fee.

An infected person, whether he goes to his
family doctor or to a public clinic will be asked
about his contacts. The physician will want to
know the name of his sex partner or partners. I
urge you to be cooperative and completely truth-
ful. This is not snitching, nor is it dishonorable.
You have a moral obligation to do what you can
to help the authorities check disease—any disease
—regardless of its nature. If you had contracted
typhoid fever, would you remain silent about the
possible carrier and permit that person to infect
others? Well, gonorrhea and syphilis are equally
infectious. And then there is always the possibility
that the person from whom *you* contracted the

disease is unaware that he is infected. Reporting him in this case would do him a favor.

This chapter has not been an easy one to write, but no book for teen-agers on the subject of sex would be worth a hoot without it.

eight

What You Should Know about Homosexuality

The subject of homosexuality is clearly a hot potato. Even in presumably enlightened circles, the word *homosexual* often produces a raised eyebrow or a snicker.

Why include this hot potato in a book for teen-agers? Because my mail tells me that thousands of teen-agers are either abysmally ignorant or have wildly cockeyed notions about the subject. They need constructive information, but they don't know where to get it. Many teen-agers who write to me expressing the fear that they might be homosexual say they would "rather die" than discuss the problem with someone they know.

In my search for background material I found pitifully little that has been written in terms a teen-ager could understand. In fact, I found pitifully little written in terms an *adult* could understand—unless he happened to be a psychiatrist.

This chapter, of course, is no scholarly study. I am neither physician nor psychiatrist. But I do think I can help substitute dangerous ignorance with a measure of understanding. And I hope to dispel some of the anxieties resulting from a problem which too long has been swept under the rug.

I have read a bale of material by the experts—

analysts, psychiatrists, physicians, sociologists and criminologists. The only point on which *all* the experts seem to agree is that there are massive disagreements among the experts.

The teen-agers who write to me seeking information and counsel on homosexuality are usually between 14 and 19 years of age. Sometimes they write about a friend they suspect is "a little queer." Or they may be concerned about a member of the family who "doesn't seem quite right." But usually they write about themselves.

About 70 percent of the letters come from boys. Most of the boys who write are tortured with guilt and self-hatred. They live on the razor's edge, terrified that someone may learn they aren't "like everybody else." Often they beg for help in the confidential section of the column, reluctant to sign their names or unwilling to risk a reply in the mail.

Many who write are so ashamed of their physical desires for members of their own sex that they speak of suicide. One 17-year-old Chicago boy wrote, "If I can't get cured I would rather kill myself than be a pansy all my life."

Then there are the letters from teen-agers who fear they may be homosexual. Often they are mistaken. It is not unnatural for a teen-ager to be especially attracted to a member of his own sex—a music teacher, a coach, a school nurse, a neighbor or someone in his own age group.

Some teen-agers have written about a single experience which they fear has made them homosexuals. The fact is, according to the experts, that an isolated experience of this kind—or even two or three such experiences—cannot make a person a homosexual. Such experimentation should be stopped, of course, because it can lead to profound anxiety, possible blackmail and long-term entanglements with undesirable people.

Before we go further perhaps we should define our terms. What is a homosexual? A homosexual is a male or female who desires, physically, members of his own sex. A female homosexual is called a Lesbian.

Is homosexuality something new? What does history say about it? Homosexuality is probably as old as man. In some cultures it has been viewed as an acceptable method of controlling the population. In societies where survival of the tribe or race depended on an increasing population, homosexuality was taboo.

Twenty-four hundred years ago homosexuality was widely practiced among the Greeks and Romans. Today there is a popular belief that homosexuality contributed, in a very important way, to the decline of both societies. The historians say not so. They tell us, instead, that in the Greek and Roman cultures of that era, women were social and intellectual inferiors—their role was that of housekeeper and child-bearer. Passionate friendships among men were considered normal. Women were not "good enough" or "sufficiently intelligent" to merit intimate relationships. Not until the Christian era was homosexuality looked upon as immoral in Western civilization.

Do all homosexuals carry out sexual procedures? No. Some homosexuals are too inhibited or fearful of the consequences.

Is it possible to tell if a person is a homosexual by looking at him? No. In some instances an overt homosexual can be identified at a glance, but generally it is not possible to make the judgment by observation.

There's a bit of folklore to the effect that most males who are creative or talented in the arts are "gay" and that a homosexual can be spotted by his effeminate walk and ladylike mannerisms. This is nonsense. Some homosexuals are artists and some homosexuals affect feminine mannerisms, but so do many normal men. On the opposite side of the coin, many male homosexuals appear to be spectacularly masculine.

There are numerous inaccurate assumptions concerning female homosexuals, as well. It is *not* true that women who excel in athletics, join the armed services, wear short haircuts and flat-heeled shoes tend to be Lesbians. While some female homosexuals fit this description, many Lesbians are feminine in appearance and dress. They can and do excite strong sexual responses in males, although they themselves have no physical desire for males. Some Lesbians who despise men enjoy arousing a male's sexual appetite and then punishing him with rejection.

Both male and female homosexuals sometimes marry and have children, in the hope that the trappings of a normal life will produce in them normal sexual drives (of course it doesn't work). But many homosexuals who marry do so to mask their homosexuality. Marriage provides a respectable cover and enables them to move about in conventional circles. These people are actually bisexual, since they are also capable of normal sexual activities. Their genuine satisfactions, however, are found with members of their own sex. I have had dozens of letters from men and women who tell me they married homosexuals and did not realize it until years later.

And now the big question: What causes homosexuality? It is on this point that the experts collide. A few authorities insist that a homosexual is a person who was "born wrong"—that he is a biological accident with a defective glandular system and an improper hormone balance.

In support of this theory they give us Exhibit A: the homosexual male with the high-pitched, girlish voice, the beardless face and the delicate features; and Exhibit B: the Lesbian with the deep voice, the masculine features and excessive hair on the face, arms and legs. "The evidence is incontestable," these experts insist. "Homosexuals are born wrong."

The view which is finding more and more acceptance is that homosexuality is a gross symptom of a serious psychological disturbance. The specialists who hold this view insist that the vast majority of homosexuals are organically normal. They do not discount, however, the possibility that a small percentage of homosexuality is due to physical defects at birth.

In rebuttal to Exhibit A and Exhibit B (those homosexuals who do indeed have glandular deficiencies and an improper hormone balance), the second group of experts points to normal males with high-pitched voices, beardless faces and effeminate features. They also point to normal females who have deep voices, masculine features and excessive hair growth. These individuals, in spite of their glandular and hormone problems, are emotionally healthy and lead normal sex lives.

From the debate one point, at least, emerges: No one knows why the emotional problems of one child may lead him to excessive thumb-sucking or prolonged bed-wetting, while another child's emotional problems may turn him into a homosexual.

Here are a few psychiatric case histories of homosexuals—examples which support the theory that homosexuality results from early childhood problems.

Harold was the only child of a domineering mother. She made all the decisions in the family, ignoring her husband as if he did not exist. Harold ignored his father, too, because he seemed inconsequential. He grew up admiring and imitating his mother since there was nothing in his father's personality or behavior which seemed worthy of imitation. Harold bore a strong physical resemblance to his mother—a blue-eyed blonde—and he was pleased when friends and relatives pointed out that he was "a spitting image of his mother." He enjoyed the identification and worked hard at duplicating his mother's mannerisms and personality. Harold's lack of respect for his father and his strong admiration of his mother motivated him to choose the female role for himself since this was the person *he* wanted to be. He remained in the role of the female throughout his life.

Roberta was the fourth girl in a family where a son was fervently wanted. They had even named her Robert before birth and disappointedly added the "a." Roberta learned early that her parents had wanted her to be a boy, so she decided to be one. She excelled in sports, went hunting and fishing with her father, rode horseback, played baseball and became an outstanding golfer. Roberta's mother paid little attention to her. She was clearly her father's pet. She wore boy's clothing whenever possible, and insisted that her friends call her "Bob." "Bob" remained in the male world where she found her satisfactions and rewards.

Gordon was a very pretty little boy. His father died when he was five months old. Gordon's mother thought he looked darling in long curls and ribbons. She dressed him like a girl "because he was so beautiful." Everyone fussed over him, and he was often mistaken for a girl. Gordon enjoyed this role because it was attention-getting, and it required nothing of him except that he look pretty and soak up adoration. As he became older he was afraid to play with boys because boys were too rough. Life was infinitely easier as a girl. Gordon took to wearing his mother's makeup and clothing. He later found sexual outlets with homosexuals who played the male role. Gordon remained the female.

Margaret's parents were rigid disciplinarians and devoutly religious. They warned her of the evils of sex and cautioned her against having anything to do with boys. Sex, they told her, was dirty and sinful. Boys were filthy and wicked. By the time Margaret was 14 years old she had developed an overwhelming aversion to boys. Margaret enjoyed hugging and kissing her girl friends because there was nothing "wicked or sinful" in such behavior. It squared with her early training. When she was 18 she became acquainted with other girls who wanted nothing to do with boys. Margaret found her sexual outlets with this group.

Vernon was the middle boy in a family of three

sons. His father favored his older brother and his mother favored his youngest brother. Vernon was suspended somewhere in the middle, competing unsuccessfully on both sides. He wanted fiercely to win his mother's affection and tried untiringly to gain her favor. He visualized his mother as the most beautiful woman in the world and at an early age imagined himself as her sweetheart. When Vernon was 10 years old he became angry with his father and threatened to "marry Mommy and take her away from him." He was given a severe beating for this outburst and warned never again to say such a horrible thing. As Vernon grew older he became aware of his physical desires for his mother but such desires, he knew, were immoral and evil so he buried them deep in his mind. He grew up thinking of *all* girls as "Mother" and was wracked with shame and guilt when he was in the presence of attractive females. By the time Vernon reached his eighteenth birthday he had made his choice. He was unable to accept a female as a sex object because all girls were "Mother," so Vernon found his sexual outlet with male companions who shared his twisted notions.

Bruce was a delicate and sickly child. He was slight of build and had effeminate features. Bruce was sexually stirred by girls but their attitude toward him was platonic. Girls found him bright and amusing but they treated him as if he were a girl friend because, unfortunately, he had few qualities which suggested masculinity. When Bruce was 16 years old his mother took him to the family physician for an examination. She was worried because his voice had not changed and he had no sign of fuzz on his face. The doctor confirmed her suspicion that Bruce had a glandular deficiency. He was put on medication. The medication helped somewhat but Bruce continued to look effeminate and his voice remained high-pitched. He dated girls and even necked with three or four, but he found life too competitive as a male. He had no chance with girls when other boys were present. His ego suffered horribly. When Bruce was 18 he gave up the battle and became "one of the girls."

All human beings go through stages when they prefer the company of members of their own sex —and it's perfectly natural. Very young children play together indiscriminately. By the time a youngster reaches six or seven years of age he usually prefers companions of his own sex. This preference may continue until high school age, varying with the individual.

It is not uncommon to see 11- and 12-year old girls holding hands or with arms around one another as they walk down the street. Girls often dance together, talk on the telephone endlessly and spend weekends in each other's homes. This is normal. These girls do not have sexual desires for one another. What they feel is a sense of companionship.

At about the age 11 or 12, girls begin to take an interest in boys. Boys usually begin to notice girls at about 14 or 15. Some boys are late starters, however, and have no interest in girls until they are 17 or even 18. The boy or girl who reaches 20 and is not attracted to the opposite sex shows the possibility of a problem personality.

Certain deviations from the norm may not involve homosexuality. One type of deviation is called transvestism. Transvestites are either men or women who find pleasure in dressing up in the clothing of the opposite sex. Some transvestites do not seek homosexual partners—they find their solitary enjoyment in the act of dressing up.

At this point I would like to make the distinction between homosexuals and child-molesters. Many adults do not know the difference. It is not true that all homosexuals are child-molesters or that they are constantly making attempts to "ruin" young boys by introducing them to their way of life. Most homosexuals stick closely to their own circle of friends and mind their own business. Child-molesters are psychopathic personalities, a serious threat to society and they should be institutionalized and treated.

Almost every boy, by the time he has reached 18 years of age, has been approached by a homosexual. Homosexuals often loiter around parks, public toilets and places where boys are apt to gather. If such an approach is made all that need be said is "I'm not interested," then leave the premises at once. There is no need for violence, anger or shame.

I've had many letters from boys who are filled with fear because a number of homosexuals have made passes at them. They are afraid something must be wrong with them or they would not attract "queers." Their fears are groundless. While something is drastically wrong with the person who makes the pass, nothing is wrong with *them*.

And now, what can be done to set the homosexual on the track of normality? First, let's not assume that all homosexuals *want* to be set on the track. Many homosexuals are content as they are and have no wish to change. They are not a problem to society or to themselves.

Most homosexuals, however, yearn to be normal. And these are the ones whose heartbreaking letters cross my desk daily. Twisted and sick, through no fault of their own, they want desperately to be "like everyone else."

What can be done for the homosexual who wants to be normal? Very little in the way of a "cure" but a great deal in terms of adjustment. Psychiatric therapy can, in most cases, give the homosexual some understanding and insight into his problem. It can help him adjust to his condition and accept himself as he is. Talking about a problem with a doctor often can be tremendously helpful.

The chances for a complete cure are slim. An optimistic estimate is that only about four out of one hundred can be made heterosexual—and then only with concentrated therapy. The chances are better, of course, if the homosexual seeks professional help in his early teens and is willing and able (and financially capable) to undertake intensive therapy.

To those of you who are reading this chapter for information only, and not because you are seeking help for yourselves, I would like to leave this thought:

Be thankful you have been blessed with healthy, normal sex drives, and remember that not all boys and girls are so fortunate. When you encounter people who are "different," remember that their lives are probably unbelievably difficult and that they are faced with the enormous problem of adjustment. You can help by understanding.

nine

Is It Sex
or the Real Thing?

What is love?

This is the 64-billion-dollar question, and as of now the jackpot is still unclaimed. Everyone wants to fall in love although no one knows for sure what it is he hopes to fall into.

Love is a favorite theme for poets, novelists and song writers. Its magic spell is supposed to be everywhere. Tons upon tons of literature have been written on the subject. Millions of people insist they've "been there" yet no one can define it. Why? Because love means something different to each of us.

The word *love* appears in every language known to man. But a careful study of the Bible and our historical heritage discloses a different employment of the word—it was applied to parents, grandparents, brothers, sisters, country and God. The romantic notion of love—the "real gone" variety—is a relatively recent invention.

Some historians say it began in the Western world in the twelfth century. Troubadors who roamed the countryside made up songs about "love." These songs had enormous appeal because they opened the door to a world of fantasy—a world where woman was pursued, adored and desired by man. This was a new idea. Today, six centuries later, every Tom, Dick and Harry, Sue, Lou and Mary hopes to be kicked in the head by that butterfly.

We are told that even though the twelfth-century lady swooned at the sight of her shining knight she rarely married him. Romantic palpitations were exciting but a quickening of the pulse was not considered a solid foundation for something as important as marriage. The fair ladies of medieval days married for practical reasons and enjoyed their romantic affairs in secret.

In some cultures romance was (and still is) considered a fringe benefit which may or may not come *after* marriage. The parents arranged for the betrothals of their sons and daughters. The bride and groom often met for the first time at their wedding ceremony. Anthropologists tell us that those marriages frequently turned out well, crediting the similarity of religious, social and financial backgrounds, plus the foregone conclusion that marriage was "forever." This doctrinaire, unsentimental formula seems cold and calculating but it proved to be a sturdier basis for a life together than our twentieth-century teen-age marriages which add up to little more than one set of glands calling out to another.

This letter from White Plains, New York, makes the point:

"Dear Ann Landers:

"My name is Randy. Maybe you will remember me by the letter I wrote to you three weeks ago. I just wanted to tell you how things turned out.

"Remember how I thought for sure I was in love? I wanted to give Dottie my class ring and my I.D. bracelet. I even wanted to buy her a $5 heart-shaped box of candy for Valentine's Day. I was like crazy, man. My head felt light as a feather. When I looked at Dottie I got weak in the knees and almost fainted. I perspired until my shirt was soaked through. My appetite was shot and I couldn't even look at food. Mom told me I looked terrible and she called the doctor.

"Well, it wasn't love at all. It was the flu. I am feeling fine now and I'm dating Dottie but I'm going with other girls, too. I just thought you might like to know I'm flying right. And thanks for your advice to simmer down and relax. I think it speeded up my recovery.

Back to Normal"

Experts in the field of marriage counseling agree that the well-advertised moon-June-croon type of love has produced more miserable marriages than happy ones. Young people (and older ones as well) who are in love with love, marry too soon and for the wrong reasons. They are swept along by free-flowing juices—unwilling to give the relationship a chance to flower and bloom.

Teen-agers who have a healthy attitude toward sex will not rush to the altar for physical reasons. They are able to put sex in its proper place. And they know its proper place is *not* at the top of the list in blazing neon lights. Some teens make the mistake of believing that being informed or knowing "the facts of life" will assure them of complete sexual compatibility in marriage. In the words of the song, "It ain't necessarily so."

Sound information is vital, but all around us we see evidence that it isn't what we *know* about sex but how we *feel* about it that counts. Knowledge and the ability to apply that knowledge to our own lives are vastly different things.

Many physicians, nurses, anatomists and biologists who should know most of what there is to know about the human body and how it functions have unsatisfactory sex lives. On the other hand an even greater number of ordinary, everyday people who have no clinical information whatever, enjoy an enormously satisfying sex life.

Sex attitudes are largely shaped in childhood. Parents who have a wholesome approach to sex are aware that a good physical relationship will glorify and strengthen their love. They pass on these healthy attitudes to their children. It need not necessarily be articulated. An atmosphere of harmony and unity warms the home.

The opposite is also true. Couples who are poorly adjusted sexually sometimes are ashamed to admit to themselves that they have such a problem. They bicker and quarrel about *other* things. She criticizes him in front of the children because he slurps his soup and leaves his socks and shoes in the living room. He finds fault with her relatives and complains that she is extravagant and spends "his" money recklessly.

The entire family suffers in any number of subtle (or not so subtle) ways. Children who are raised in homes where anxiety and hostility are part of their daily lives often bring to their own marriages the same destructive qualities. A recent study on divorce suggested that the child of divorced parents is three times as likely to have a divorce of his own as the child whose home remains whole.

Some children grow up in families where sex is never mentioned. These children get the idea there must be something drastically wrong with physical love. An inhibited or self-conscious parent who is unable to discuss sex or even answer a child's questions, is himself so emotionally crippled that his child must look elsewhere for guidance and counsel.

I've received letters from teen-agers whose parents *have* talked to them about sex—and with shattering results. Mothers who fear and despise sex make certain their daughters are adequately warned against this "monstrous evil." Here are a few samples from my mail:

Lexington, Kentucky:

"My mother says all men are animals and they are after only one thing. I have dated some very nice fellows and I can't imagine any of them acting like animals. My mother says they pretend to be decent and polite at first, but it's only an act. When they get girls to fall for them they turn into beasts."

From Providence, Rhode Island:

"I've read novels about love and marriage and it all sounds so heavenly. My mother says it's a lie. She says sex is only enjoyable for men. Women just have to put up with it."

Boys unburden themselves, too. Here is a letter from Boston:

> "I am 15 and an honor student. My father took me aside last night and asked me if I had made a girl, yet. I told him no. He said when he was my age he had been around plenty and he hoped there wasn't anything wrong with me. He ordered me to get my nose out of the books and go out and learn what life is all about. Maybe there *is* something wrong with me. I have no desire to make a girl. In fact the thought of it sort of scares me."

Where do parents get such twisted notions?

If sex is never mentioned in your home or worse yet, if your parents have told you that sex is vulgar, disgusting or sinful, I urge you to retool your thinking.

Let's start at the beginning. All of us have some mixed feelings about sex. As Robert Louis Stevenson said, "We all have feelings inside that would shame hell." And if your thoughts are tinged with guilt don't rush to the conclusion that you are hopelessly warped and evil-minded. Our society has triggered these conflicts and we must learn how to live with them.

For example, when we were small children we were permitted to romp about without clothing. Almost every family album has pictures of tiny ones wearing only a sweet smile. When we emerge from the toddling stage we are instructed to keep parts of our bodies covered because it's "naughty" to be exposed. Anthropologists tell us that in cultures where people wear no clothing there are relatively few emotionally disturbed people.

But obviously, nudity is not our alternative, because the wearing of clothing is built into the historic convention of our society. While the anthropological testimony cited above is incontestable, it applies to people who have dramatically different cultural roots.

When we reach adolescence our feelings of ambivalence and conflict become greater. We experience drives to translate our sexual desires into action. We know, however, that this is against the moral code, that it involves all sorts of risks, so we tell ourselves that we must keep our passions under control. It's not easy. Nature plays a mean trick by allowing the physical urges and strong desires to come years before we are emotionally or financially ready for marriage.

It is not possible to erase from memory the concepts we learned as children. We cannot unlearn what we have learned. But we *can* replace secondrate notions with better ones. We can remodel our attitudes and apply the remodeled attitudes to our lives.

Begin with this concept of sex and you will have an excellent start: *Sex is one of God's most generous gifts.*

We are born with sex drives just as we are born with drives to satisfy hunger and thirst. God meant sex to be pleasurable, beautiful, filled with wonder and rich in reward. But it can be pleasurable, beautiful and rewarding only if it is used properly. You wouldn't take a diamond and platinum brooch to try to pry open a jar of pickles with it, would you? Using sex in the wrong way adds up to the same thing.

God designed the sex act to be a marvelously enjoyable experience because He wanted to insure procreation. The primary purpose of sex is to perpetuate the human race.

But as a purely physical act sex makes no contribution to our emotional well-being. Too often sex and love are used interchangeably. The expression "to make love" may or may not involve tender and beautiful feelings of reciprocation. When it is only a selfish adventure in pleasure, with no concern for the other person, it is not making love, it is making sex. And this is one of the reasons intercourse outside of marriage is usually hollow and unrewarding for both partners. Such lovemaking is completely self-centered. The motivation for out-of-bounds sex is to get—not to give.

Sex cannot be separated from the total personality. The mature person fortunate enough to have a generally healthy attitude toward his fellow human beings will probably have a healthy sex life. The person who has difficulty adjusting to new situations, who cannot get along with neighbors, bosses or colleagues, who is fearful, suspicious, selfish, demanding, timid or domineering, will bring his personality problem to the bedroom.

An overly aggressive and egotistical man who exploits his friends, relatives and business associates will undoubtedly exhibit these aggressive and exploitive qualities in his sex life. The person who is considerate, unselfish and generous in his interpersonal relations in all probability will behave in the same thoughtful and considerate manner behind closed doors.

Then there are women who use sex as a weapon. They withhold themselves from a man until, in exchange for their "love," they can get something they want. Such abuse of sex is a form of prostitution. It is not giving—it's trading.

When sexual incompatibility is given as the cause for divorce, it is almost a certainty that the couple got along poorly in other areas as well. Unsatisfactory sex relations are a manifestation of other deficiencies. The following lines describe such situations well:

"My husband is so tight with money you wouldn't believe it. I don't have one penny I can call my own. He goes to the market with me every Friday and I could die of embarrassment. He takes things out of the basket right in front of the checker and says, 'We don't need these luxuries. I'm not made out of money, you know.' Then he turns around the very next day and spends $200 on fishing equipment for himself. He complains because my love-making is 'mechanical.' He calls me a cold tomato. How can a woman get steamed up over a man who is selfish and inconsiderate?"

But it's a two-way street, and I'm sorry to say the traffic is fairly heavy. Here is a letter from a husband:

"My wife complains because I'm not romantic any more. She's right. I'm not. But if you could see the way she slops around the house in a dirty bathrobe for days at a time you'd understand why. I've asked her a million times to please comb her hair and wash her face before I come home at night, but I might as well talk to the wall. She has gained 35 pounds since we married 10 years ago and every dress she owns is splitting apart at the seams. The house is always a mess and I wouldn't dare invite my business friends over. She hates to cook so we eat out of tin cans or cartons from the delicatessen. Her laziness has killed my love for her. Of course I'm not romantic any more. Why should I be?"

When such couples seek a divorce the collapse of the marriage is often blamed on sexual incompatibility—they fail to realize it was the symptom rather than the cause.

How important is sex in marriage? Pretty darned important. But it isn't everything. A marriage without sex would, of course, be sterile and empty. But couples who communicate only physically learn to their bitter disappointment that sex alone is an unreliable adhesive agent. It won't hold a marriage together.

Many girls who dream of marital bliss envision themselves hour after hour in the bedroom—lolling about in chiffon and lace. There's no similarity between this Hollywood image and what actually happens. No relationship between two people can remain at fever-pitch forever. And it's fortunate indeed, or we'd be nervous wrecks. Business pressures, the demands of running a home and caring for children, periods of anxiety and tension often reduce sexual energy—and it's to be expected.

To the thousands of young people who write to me and ask how to distinguish between sexual attraction and the real thing I say this:

Ask yourself—how do you feel about the total person? Do you admire and respect him? Is his word good or are his promises written on flowing water and shifting sand? Do you *like* him as well as love him? Is he your friend? Is he willing to put your desires before his own—or do you find yourself catering to *his* every wish and whim?

What can you share? Do you have common interests, common goals, and are you pulling in the same direction? Do you understand that his profession or his job may draw heavily on his time and energy? Are you willing to help him in his work by being cooperative and patient?

Many a man has been wrecked professionally because his wife considered his career a competing mistress. Loving means giving, and often it means giving him the moral support he needs to do his job so he can share with you feelings of achievement and self-respect.

How important is necking to your total relationship? Must you neck every time you get together, or can you spend some evenings just talking? Do you need other people around to insure an evening of fun? Or can the two of you have a stimulating and interesting time alone?

Are you at ease with him—relaxed and comfortable in his presence? Or do you find yourself playing a part, straining to keep his approval, fearful that perhaps you may say the wrong thing?

Examine the quality of your arguments. (If two people agree on everything, one of them is unnecessary.) Argument is healthy. It clears the air. A marriage which cannot tolerate differences in opinion is not a marriage but a dictatorship. Arguments can be destructive, however, if the individuals attack each other instead of the issue.

Can you be objective about the one you have chosen? A great many romanticists are hopelessly in love with an image which bears little resemblance to the real person. This is why, when people write and insist it was "love at first sight," I suggest that they calm down and take a second look. There is no such thing as love at first sight. Some of those attractive first-sight qualities may turn out to be genuine and durable, but don't count on the storybook formula.

The other bromide, "love is blind," is far more sensible. The young girl (or even the older one) who believes herself to be in love cannot see the undesirable qualities in her man because she wishes *not* to see them. To her, he is the handsomest, brightest, smoothest, sweetest, most adorable man in all the world. Perhaps his professors or his boss or his roommate may consider him irresponsible, ugly-tempered, lazy or stupid but she sees it not at all.

Time is your best ally in evaluating an individual's true character and measuring your compatibility. No one can play a part forever. The mask must fall sooner or later. It is for this reason that I plead with the teen-agers who write to me, to *wait*. Don't rush into marriage immediately upon graduation from high school or worse yet—before. The artificial conditions under which most teen-agers date do not allow for the opportunity to observe one another under a variety of circumstances. Too many are on their best behavior and the stage on which they are performing bears little resemblance to the world in which they must live once they're married.

And now the big question: How can you tell if it is love or sex?

Let these be your guideposts:

Sex is purely physical. Love is emotional, spiritual *and* physical. You must touch minds as well as bodies if your relationship is to be fulfilling and meaningful. Love is friendship that has caught fire. It must take root and grow—one day at a time. Those who indulge in sex for sheer excitement and physical pleasure get exactly what they bargained for, and nothing more. After the fleeting moments of pleasure, they are spent and empty.

The perfect love experience is communication in its most complete and selfless sense. It frees us from the prison of our aloneness and makes us whole, sharing ineffably tender moments—sharing and giving. Love can be the strongest force in all the world...Hercules unchained.

I hope that all of you someday will know this most exquisite of all experiences, the moment when you give your most precious gift—yourself— to your beloved in marriage. You will be glad you waited, and you will be ever thankful that you refused to settle for a shoddy substitute.

ten

From You to Me

I've received thousands of letters like this.

"Dear Ann Landers:

"The first letter in your column today really hit me between the eyes. That letter could have been written by me. Your answer shook me up plenty. But more important, it prevented me from making a big mistake. Thanks a lot."

These letters are solid testimony that people often recognize their own problems when they are reading about the problems of others. We *do* learn from the mistakes of others, and it's a good thing, because we don't live long enough to make 'em all ourselves.

I don't believe in preaching to kids. In the first place it doesn't work. Nobody changes anybody. People *can* and *do* change, but the changes must be made voluntarily, from within.

Let's face it, no one likes to be told what to do. It's human nature to bristle at an order and balk at a command. All of us respond best to suggestion. While reading about the problems of others, and taking note of the advice that follows, you may pick up an idea or two. One such idea may save a peck of trouble.

Each of the other chapters in this book deals with a specific problem area. I have attempted to select for chapter themes those problems which are most common among teen-agers, those problems you may be reluctant to discuss with someone you know.

This chapter, however, is a dialogue between teen-age America and Ann Landers. You will encounter a number of heartaches, some not earthshaking perhaps, but rough enough to bug some teen-ager to the point where he sat down and wrote a letter about it. Here you may find answers to some of the questions which have been nagging at you. And finally, you may experience a sense of relief—just from knowing that some teen-ager, thousands of miles away has the very same problem. And perhaps that teen-ager isn't thousands of miles away at all. He may be right next door.

"Dear Ann Landers:

"You seem to think double-dating is a good idea for teen-agers. I'd like to point out that after what happened to me I don't think I'll ever double-date again.

"Gary and I teamed up with another couple Saturday night because Gary's car was in the shop. The couple we doubled with are a pair of squares. We parked just to talk and Gary kissed me a few times. This girl kept turning around in the front seat saying, 'Oh, pardon me.'

"Monday morning Miss Blabbermouth went around school telling everybody Gary and I were necking up a storm in the back seat and that I was a make-out. I say six or seven kisses is O.K. on a Saturday night date and that making out is *more* than kissing. Please print this in the paper and explain the difference. Our whole high school is waiting.

Miss Q"

"Dear Miss Q and Her Whole High School:

"When I was a teen-ager—back before the earth's crust cooled—necking was the word we used and it meant kissing, and *only* kissing.

"The term 'making out' popped up during World War II—from where no one can really prove. I can guess, however (and it's only a guess), that one soldier would ask a buddy when he returned from a weekend pass, 'How did you make out?'

"Among high school and college kids, making out can mean anything from holding hands to going the whole route.

"Beginning in the middle teens, most youngsters go in for some kissing and anyone who thinks otherwise is kidding himself. But a kiss should have significance—not any old place with anyone handy just because it's dark. A kiss should be a very special expression of affection and does not need an audience.

"A girl who is called a make-out by her friends would do well to take stock of herself."

"Dear Ann Landers:

"A short time ago a girl in the local high school had a baby out of wedlock. She was not wild or promiscuous. It was just a case of going too steadily, and too seriously, with the same boy.

"This unfortunate girl has a younger sister who is a close friend of my daughter. They belong to the same youth group. The group is having a dance in April and the girls must ask the boys. The sister invited two boys and they both turned her down. They told her they had nothing against her but that their parents forbade them to go with her because of what happened to her sister.

"The poor girl is heartsick. She has even considered quitting school. Do you see any justification whatever for the actions of the parents? I'm too involved to evaluate the situation properly. Please comment.

Mrs. J. R."

"Dear Mrs. J. R.:

"I see no justification whatsoever. The action of these parents is shocking.

"To punish an innocent girl for something her sister did is not only cruel but senseless. If this is the standard of justice the parents are setting for their sons I feel sorry for all of them."

"Dear Ann Landers:

"I'm a very unhappy girl who will be 16 in September. I've always been grown-up for my age and I started to date when I was 12. I guess you'd call me popular because I have always had more dates than I could accept. (Some nights I go out with one fellow from 7 to 10 p.m. and another one from 10 to 1 a.m.)

"I'm beginning to worry about my reputation. It seems that the very first time I go out with a guy he tries to paw me. I have necked with a few fellows, I'll admit, but I am not interested in making friends with the whole school through the Braille system. Please tell me how I can protect my reputation.

Popular But Decent"

"Dear P. but D.:

"One way to protect your reputation is to cut out the second shift. A girl who has to stagger the traffic suggests that she needs more company than sounds respectable.

"No doubt a few of the boys have been performing as publicity agents. Try a new approach—hands off, one and all. And don't go out with every fellow who asks for a date. Being selective can do wonders for your reputation."

"Dear Ann Landers:

"I'm a fella, 16, who has been outsmarted by a fifteen-year-old chick. Please tell me how to vacate Boobsville.

"We've had four live dates and I enjoy this doll's company a lot. But when we get to her front door she gives me a handshake like in the Epworth League. Before I know it she's inside the house and I'm on the outside with the door in between.

"The guys at school are giving me the har-de-har-har. They say she's taking me for a ride. Most guys in my crowd get a great goodnight kiss after two dates, or for sure by the third date. How much longer do you think I ought to stand for this brotherly farewell stuff before I tell her to get lost?

Beeswax"

"Dear Beez:

"If a girl does not dissolve in your arms after two dates it doesn't prove that you're either a failure or a sap. It could mean that she has high standards and refuses to pay for her dates with kisses.

"This chick sounds like someone who is worth taking out the fifth time, and the sixth and seventh."

"Dear Ann:

"I'm 16 and finding it not so sweet. The fellow I'm going with is 18 and a real dream wagon. The trouble is, he's not satisfied with a little light pitching. He says I've kept him in line for four months and that's long enough. He claims I've proven I'm a nice girl and now I can be normal and stop acting like Queen Victoria.

"Last night we were parked on a lonely road and got into a terrible fight over the same old thing. He said the hard-to-get routine is all right 'for awhile,' but that I was overdoing it. The last thing he said was, 'I'm fed up with the broken record.' I like him *very* much and don't want to lose him. What shall I do now?

Too Pure?"

"Dear Too:

"That broken record produces darned fine music. Just keep telling him to behave himself ... behave himself ... behave himself ... behave himself."

"Dear Ann Landers:

"When are girls going to get smart and

demand the same standard of virtue that the boys demand of them?

"The guy who wants to play around with tramps while he's dating and then expects a good girl when he's 'ready for something important like marriage' ought to be sent to the bargain basement right along with the girls he helped to put there.

"I've been talking this way for a long time, Ann. When I was in high school, girls told me I'd never find a boy with standards that high. But I found him, and I married him, and I'll wager he is more manly than those creeps who had so much 'proving' to do before marriage.

"I'm sure I didn't get the only good guy in the world. There must be others left. Happy hunting, girls.

Mrs. Lucky"

"Dear Lucky:

"Not all boys demand white-flower girls for marriage, but those who make such demands should have unsullied records themselves."

"Dear Ann Landers:

"I am a girl 17 who wears glasses. I'm dating a fellow who also wears glasses. He is rather shy and I know he has wanted to kiss me a couple of times but so far he has not managed to get around to it.

"Last night he leaned over to kiss me and his glasses bumped mine. He said, 'excuse me' —and changed his mind. We have a date next weekend. Do you think it would be too bold if I take my glasses off later in the evening when I don't have to see where I am going?

Glass Menagerie"

"Dear Menagerie:

"When a girl removes her glasses it does not always add up to an invitation to be kissed. It could mean that she merely wishes to massage the bridge of her nose. Doesn't the bridge of your nose ever need massaging —late in the evening, that is, when you don't have to see where you're going?"

"Dear Ann:

"I am a high school senior and I've laughed my head off at some of the troubles you've printed but if you can help me I'll never laugh again.

"My problem is my steady girl. She thinks the front seat of my car is a sofa and that I'm a chair. If she isn't almost on my lap, her arms are wrapped around my neck. She distracts me and sometimes blocks my vision. After a few close calls I have pleaded with her to please let me drive the car with both hands. She says four eyes are better than two hands and that she is always on the lookout.

"If I have an accident I'll be grounded for life. My Dad is strict about the car (it's his) and I get it only as long as I have a perfect record. Help me, please.

Buzzy"

"Dear Buzzy:

"Tell that shy octopus that 40 eyes are of no value unless the driver's two hands and two feet are free to act in a split second. Give her these alternatives: Either she stays over on her side of the seat or you'll both have to travel by bus or be pedestrians."

"Dear Ann Landers:

"The letter from 'Fourth Choice' hit home. The anti-make-outs were unhappy because they had no dates. They said the fast girls were rushed to death. Well, Ann, I'm one of the fast girls, and I'd like to tell you how it looks from here.

"I get asked out every night of the week and I'm sick of these creeps who want to make out all the time. I am also sick of myself. I'm only 17 and my reputation isn't worth a plugged nickel. My girl friends tell me what they hear about me from their brothers and of course I deny everything. I know now that nine guys out of ten can't be trusted to keep their mouths shut. Whenever I meet a new fellow I wonder how much he has heard.

"Please tell 'Fourth Choice' that I wish I could change places with her.

Too Late for Me"

"Dear Too Late:

"I agree with your letter but I don't agree with your signature. Even a sordid experience can be valuable if you learn from it. Now that you realize what a foolish girl you've been, resolve to cut out the nonsense. Easy? No—but it can be done."

"Dear Ann Landers:

"When you spoke at our high school you said, 'The girl is the big loser in the game of heavy romance.' Well, I'd like to tell you that the boy can be a big loser, too. I know because I am one who is.

"My girl is 15. I am 17. We started going steady two years ago which was our first big mistake. The more time we spent together the easier it was to go a little further. Before we knew it we were doing things we had no right to do. We made up all kinds of excuses to justify our behavior—even that old line about living every day to the limit because tomorrow we might be hit by an H-bomb.

"Then my girl found out for sure that she was in trouble. I'll never forget the agony of telling our parents. They were so shocked and hurt. It was the most horrible experience a couple of kids can go through.

"Now my girl is in another city with relatives. Our parents have decided it would be best if we didn't write or see each other. The baby will be put out for adoption. I don't know how my girl will feel about me when all this is over. All I can say now is that I am heartsick and miserable.

More My Fault Than Hers"

"Dear More:

"Too bad you had to learn the tough way. At this point I can only offer you my sympathy."

"Dear Ann Landers:

"Your cornball advice is making me sick to my stomach. When teen-age girls write and ask how to be popular why don't you level with them instead of dishing out that slop about being loyal, friendly, interesting and 'fun to be with.'

"Anybody whose skull is on straight knows that the way to be popular is to have a rich father so you can live in a beautiful home and buy the latest gone platters for your stereo. It also helps if you have a new convertible. If a girl doesn't have any of this she absolutely must have a beautiful face or at least knockout measurements.

"So muffle that eighteenth-century draw-

ing-room rattle, Granny Landers, and give
the cats the hip scoop.

Sapphire Needle"

"Dear Needle:

"I receive plenty of letters from girls who
are sitting in their lovely homes—alone—
with their beautiful faces and knockout measurements, listening to the gone platters. The
kids are gone, too. They left when they became bored. And it didn't take long.

"The way to have friends is to make people
want to be around you. It takes warmth and
sparkle. The expensive trappings may attract
a few bees, but they sip the honey and fly
away."

"Dear Ann Landers:

"My father is like a dictator. He thinks a
girl 15 is an infant. Two weeks ago the kids
had a beer-bust on the beach. Dad said I
couldn't go because the Saturday before I got
in too late. (Ike's car broke down.) When I
told Ike I couldn't go to the beer-bust, he said
he'd come over to see me. I knew my old
man wouldn't let him in the house because I
was supposed to be in solitary, so I told Ike
to climb in through my bedroom window.

"About 10:30 we heard my dad coming
down the hall so Ike got under my bed. Our
dog was under the bed and Ike must have

stepped on him. Anyway the dog yelped and Ike had had it.

"Now I'm grounded for a month. Do you realize this is four miserable, lousy weeks? I'll crack up. How can I get my dad to trust me?

Stalag 17"

"Dear Stalag:

"Trust must be earned—and it must be earned one day at a time by consistently honorable behavior.

"I'm not surprised you're in hot water, Toots. No honorable girl would invite her boy friend to sneak into the house through the bedroom window and hide under the bed. If you want to be treated like an honest, mature person, cut out the angle-shooting and play it straight."

"Dear Ann Landers:

"I'm 18 and in love with a boy who is also 18. I graduated from high school last June. For reasons I won't go into, Boris won't be graduating until next June.

"Last Christmas he gave me an engagement ring. When my folks saw it they asked me when we planned to be married. I told them in about six or eight years. They raised Cain and made me give the ring back.

"I have a good job and I'm saving money

toward our marriage. Boris has a part-time job and he bought himself a car to run around in. My main complaint is that he never cared much about going to church before he met me. And he drinks a little too much. With my help he is showing signs of reforming. I love him and think we could be happy. Do you?

Don't Know"

"Dear Little Girl:

"What you 'Don't Know' would fill several large volumes. I'll just hit some of the high spots:

(1) An 18-year-old girl who ties herself up for six or eight years has rocks in her head.

(2) A high school kid who 'doesn't care much about church' and 'drinks a little too much' is bad news.

(3) A girl who saves money toward marriage while her boy friend buys himself a car 'to run around in' is a fool. She usually winds up supporting both herself and her husband while he blows whatever he makes on extras.

"You need this infant like a moose needs a hat rack. Forget him."

"Dear Ann Landers:

"I'm 17 and feel like a big failure in life. A certain fellow I know is absolutely the dream of every girl in school. Well, it finally happened. He asked for a date. I was in my glory. The next night he came over and we went for a ride. He said he was in love with me and wanted me to be his girl. I don't know what came over me, but I lost all my will-power. I was putty in his hands and you can guess the rest.

"He didn't call me the next day like he promised. Two days passed and he still didn't call. I couldn't stand it any longer so I called him. He said he was busy with his boat and would see me soon.

"I've seen him at parties, at a ball game and on the street. He says 'Hi,' and goes right on. Please don't bawl me out, Ann. I know what I did was wrong and also stupid. It didn't help me to keep the boy! It helped me to lose him. What I want to know is, *why?* After all, I did what he wanted me to. Please explain.

The Phool"

"Dear Phool:

"The boy feels guilty and ashamed. He wants to forget what happened. When he sees you he's reminded, so naturally he avoids you. We all like people who bring out the best in us. You made this boy think poorly of him-self as well as you."

"Dear Ann Landers:

"I'm an 18-year-old girl and very worried.

Maybe there's something wrong with me. Kissing bores me. I've gone with some awfully handsome fellows and the thought of being kissed is thrilling. But then when it actually happens, it's a real letdown. In fact, I'd rather think about being kissed than kiss.

"Do I sound like some kind of a nut? I haven't told this to anyone because I'm afraid they will think I'm a weirdo. The first kissing I ever saw was in the movies when I was about eight years old and nothing in real life has measured up to it. Do I need a head-doctor?

Cold Lips"

"Dear Cold Lips:

"Anticipation is sometimes more exquisite than realization—especially if the build-up has been particularly glamorous. Your childhood fantasies were probably so exciting that no real-life guy could possibly live up to the dream version.

"In the next year if you are still bored, it may be wise to consult a psychiatrist and seek to conquer the problem."

"Dear Ann Landers:

"I know you are not a doctor, but I couldn't talk to a man about this so please try to help me. I am 17 years old and I'm built like an ironing board.

"I have heard of creams and oils but I'm not sure they do any good. I have also heard of an operation where a surgeon can insert paraffin cups. I would even be willing to have the operation if I thought it would help me be more attractive to fellows.

"I've only had four dates in my life and I'm sure this is the reason. What boy wants to take out a girl who has no shape at all? Please tell me what to do.

Dateless"

"Dear Dateless:

"The creams and oils do a lot of good—for the companies that sell them. I have never heard of a cream or an oil that added inches to a bustline. As for surgery, you'll have to see your doctor—but I'd strongly oppose such radical measures.

"I don't know what kind of fellows you are trying to attract, but if they go looking for dates with a tape measure they aren't worth bothering about. I suspect your real problem is a flat personality."

"Dear Ann Landers:

"I am 16, a junior in high school and a real flop. No fellow has ever asked me out a second time. There must be something wrong with me. When I'm getting dressed for a date I'm all excited and can think of a million

things to talk about. The minute I'm alone
with a guy I freeze up and wish I were home.

"My girl friends keep asking why Pat,
Herb or Dick never called back. I lie and
say they *did* call but that I didn't like them
well enough to accept another date.

"Please, Ann, how can I develop an interesting personality and not bore a guy to
death? I feel like a great big nothing.

Flopsville"

"Dear Flopsville:

"I have yet to meet a fellow who was bored
when a girl fastened her large eyes on him
and encouraged him to talk about himself.
This formula is older than the Rocky Mountains and it never fails.

"It may take as many as three questions
before the guy will unwind the story of his
life. Get a fellow to talk about Number One,
and he'll think you are the most interesting
person in the world."

"Dear Ann Landers:

"I'm a teen-ager who wants to make a success of my life. I think you can help me by ex-
plaining a few things.

"I hear a great many adults talk about us
teen-agers in generalities, as if you could
lump us all together and hang a label on us.
I feel this is unfair. All teen-agers are not

reckless drivers, speed demons and make-outs. Some of us are serious, reasonably well-behaved, and we want to make the world a better place for everyone.

"But how do we do it? I once wrote to you for advice and you stressed the importance of each individual making as much of himself as he can. You said, 'Make *you* your central project. Strive toward maturity.' I must confess I don't know what maturity is. If you can explain this one word, Ann, it may unlock other mysteries. Please try.

Hope For Tomorrow"

"Dear Hope:

"Maturity is many things. First, it's the ability to base a judgment on the Big Picture—the Long Haul. It means being able to pass up fun-for-the-minute and select the course of action which will pay off later. One of the characteristics of infancy is the 'I want it *now*' approach. Grown-up people can wait.

"Maturity is the ability to stick with a project or a situation until it is finished. The adult who is constantly changing jobs, changing friends—and changing mates—is immature. He cannot stick it out because he is not grown-up. Everything seems to 'turn sour' after awhile.

"Maturity is the capacity to face unpleasantness, frustration, discomfort and defeat without complaint or collapse. The mature person knows he can't have everything his own way. Nobody wins 'em all. He can defer to circumstances, to other people—and to time.

"Maturity is the ability to do what is expected of you, and this means being dependable. It means keeping your word. And dependability equates with personal integrity. Do you mean what you say—and do you say what you mean?

"The adult world is filled with people who can't be counted on. People who never seem to come through in the clutches. People who break promises and substitute alibis for performance. They show up late—or not at all. They are confused and disorganized. Their lives are a chaotic maze of unfinished business.

"Maturity is the ability to make a decision, and then to stick with it, riding out whatever storms may follow. This calls for clear thinking, backed with the courage to stand by your position, once you've taken it. Immature people spend their lives exploring endless possibilities and then doing nothing. Action requires courage. And there is no maturity without courage.

"Maturity is the ability to harness your abilities and your energies and do more than is expected of you. The mature person refuses to settle for mediocrity. He would rather aim high and miss the mark, than aim low —and make it."

*